VR

By
Andy Lancaster

For Abby and Aidan

Cartoons by Federico Gaggero via federico.gaggero@gmail.com

Cover illustration by Adeeba Sial via https://www.fiverr.com

ISBN: 978-1-4466-5728-7

9 781446 657287

The Plot

VR-A

The Dreamer

<FILE> <NEW>. The word processor software sprang to life and presented a blank new page on the screen. The boy working at the computer, an impressive hi-spec gaming one, was Victor Rostrun, always known as Vic.

The past few months had been so remarkable that it was impossible to know where to start. The new page looked intimidatingly empty. It was like starting a school project that you had been dreading, but eventually you just had to begin.

But, how on earth could he begin to explain the events that had taken place? Now that things were back to normal, if life could ever be normal again, the circumstances needed recording for all time. If nothing else, it was important that future generations of the family could reflect on the incredible events that had happened.

Perhaps the report should be buried in a time capsule in the garden. Then, centuries later, when the unbelievable and slightly weird things that he had just experienced were as a common place as watching television, someone could dig it up and find out when they first occurred.

And, because of the nature of those events, it seemed fitting that the task should be undertaken on the very computer that had been at the centre of the incredible circumstances.

But despite the tremendous technology that now resided in his bedroom, there was nothing remarkable about Vic.

He was small, and his hair was neither long, nor short, nor styled. His eyes were a greenish blue and he had no particular distinguishing marks that would be noted on one of those police crime pictures shown on TV. But, then again Vic was a good lad, so he would never end up as a suspect in an identity parade. His grades at school were normally average and he was never picked for the first team in sports. In fact, he could easily get lost in a crowd, and, because of his height, quite literally.

But this ordinary boy now had an extraordinary story to tell, an account of explorations of distant countries and feats of breath-taking heroism. He had completed a quest that would have caused any medieval knight to shake and clatter in his chain mail and armour. Above all that was the mind-blowing technology that he had stumbled upon, that had made it all possible.

Having gathered his thoughts, Vic flexed his fingers and began to tap on the keyboard.

"To whoever may read this.

I'm sure you have had times when it's hard to tell whether what is going on is a dream or reality. You know when you are awake but feel a bit out of it. It's like when you are sitting at school, listening to a teacher droning on. You feel woozy and it's really hard to focus. Sometimes you wonder whether you are really there in the classroom.

Or there are those times when it feels like you have been somewhere before, although you know you haven't. Or you seem to know exactly what is about to happen even though it hasn't yet! Or you have a dream at night that seems so real that when you wake up you believe the thing has actually taken place.

Well, my whole life has been like that for months!

It's been amazing, wacky, and completely mind-blowing. People would not have believed what was going on, even if I had chosen to tell them. It has been virtually impossible to work out what has been real and what may have been my imagination – which I know can sometimes be a bit wacky.

But either way, my life will never be the same, not since ..."

"Vic!", a voice called up from downstairs, "Are you still messing around on that computer? It's gone 10.30pm and you have school tomorrow. I'll be up in two minutes, and I expect to find you in bed!"

"Flip!" thought Vic to himself "I've been on here for hours again."

He quickly saved his work, shut down the computer and dived for cover under his duvet. Seconds later, the door opened. He was deliberately facing away from the beautiful pine door, burying his face in his luxurious pillows, faking a deep sleep.

A few months on, he was still trying to get used to the lovely new house and his amazing new bedroom.

He heard footsteps pad over and then his chrome bedside lamp clicked off. He opened one eye and could see the room lit by the pale blue light of his new combination clock, radio, and hot chocolate maker. The door closed with a scraping noise on the deep pile carpet that would not be out of place in the most ostentatious palace. It was so new that you left footprints in it as you walked around.

When the coast was clear, Vic looked up and gazed round the room.

Now, this was what he called a bedroom, not like the one he had had to put up with for the last few years. His old one used to have a grey linoleum floor with a small threadbare rug. It had always been so cold in the winter with the old-fashioned wooden sash windows. His curtains used to sway as the icy breeze blew through the cracks.

He flopped back on the huge pillows and considered what he would have typed next, had he not been interrupted. And, as his thoughts ran wild, he lapsed into a deep sleep and the astonishing events of the past months were played back to him vividly in his dreams.

* * *

"Rostrun!" The voice bellowed so violently that those around saw Vic leap off his chair. "Wake up you dreamer and pay attention!"

At once, Vic shook his head a couple of times and entered reality. He immediately remembered that it was a reality that he would rather have ignored. It was a Friday afternoon history lesson with the worst teacher at Alderman Roberts School - 'Pop-out' Parsons.

If that was not bad enough, it was the day on which the term's project on 'The Egyptians' were being returned. Vic always dreaded this procedure as 'Pop-out' relished the opportunity to humiliate as many pupils as possible. And after many years of practice, he was good at it.

Even if your work was good, it was never quite good enough. 'Pop-out' could always find something to pick a hole in. He often complained that the spacing between your words was too large, which wasted paper and reduced the size of the world's rainforests. And, if it was bad! Well, if you can think of the most embarrassing thing that could ever happened to you – such as accidentally wetting your pants when singing a solo on stage in front of six thousand celebrities – well Parsons could easily make you feel ten times worse!

In Alderman Roberts School folklore, it was hard to trace when the term 'Pop-out' came into being. He had taught at the school ever since it had opened, which probably accounted for the musty smell that hung around him. The nickname may well have been the idea of the first pupil who encountered his wrath, decades ago.

But now, every pupil knew the reason for the name. It was all to do with a peculiar transformation that happened to Parson's eyes when he lost his temper.

As he became angry, a state into which he frequently ascended, his eyes began to swell. Then, as he became more furious, they turned bloodshot, and the pupils disappeared into pinprick dots. Finally, when in full-blown rage his eyeballs appeared to extend on stalks, like a cartoon character that had its head slammed in a window.

Every pupil called Mr Parsons 'Pop-out', though never to his face. The thought of doing that was something that even Vic would not dare dream about.

There was a school rumour of a new boy called Rick Ward. On his first day, a group of older pupils sent him on a treacherous errand to ask Mr 'Pop-out' for some paper. Not knowing better, and thinking that was the teacher's real name, he walked boldly into Parson's classroom and carried out the task to the letter. "Please Mr Pop-out

4

...", he began. Apparently, he was never seen again although his PE bag hung on its hook for months!

Absolutely no one messed with Parsons.

As 'Pop-out' approached, Vic realised he must have been daydreaming and had missed most of the project returns. That in itself was a grave sin, but worse trouble was to come.

When 'Pop-out' reached his desk, there was no means of escape. Vic could only imagine what a chicken must feel like when cornered by a ravenous fox in a hen house, trembling in fear at the imminent kill.

Parsons stooped so his face was close to Vic's – far too close for comfort.

Vic noticed a pulsating purple vein on the side of 'Pop-out's' neck as his blood pressure soared. He bared his yellow teeth and Vic caught a whiff of foul fish.

The rant took its normal course beginning so quietly that you had to strain your ears to hear. Then after a rapid crescendo it peaked at a deafening level, and it was at this point that you could feel your hair moving under the force of the stinking blast.

(Firstly quiet) "Ah, Rostrun's project! Class, do you know that in all the years that I have taught in this hallowed academic institution ..." (Now louder - eyes swelling) "... I have never seen a piece of work as poor as this miserable offering ..." (Now loud - eyes bloodshot) "It looks like you used a nursery book to research the topic and your presentation is woeful ..." (Now very loud - pin prick pupils) "A gerbil could write more neatly than this ..." (All the class laughed nervously for fear of being seen not to appreciate the poor joke) "I have no option but to award you the lowest possible mark ..." (yelling – with eyes on stalks) "E MINUS!"

An icy mist descended on the room. To get an 'E' was bad enough, but a 'minus' meant that you had made no effort. You might as well have handed in a blank sheet of paper. All minus marks were recorded for all time in your file kept by Mrs Fussington, the ancient wrinkly old secretary, who ran the school office.

The shame of getting an E minus was almost as great as you would experience in medieval times when someone would walk in front of you ringing a bell and shouting "Unclean, unclean" to show that you had caught the plague.

Vic's reaction surprised him.

At first, he could feel his teeth grinding in anger. Then, as he stared at 'Pop-out's' hideous face, he imagined himself picking up his pen and sticking it with some force right up Parson's left nostril. There it was in his daydream, lodged half in and half out, with bogey juice slowly dribbling down the pen towards the nib. Then, to the wild cheering of his classmates he stuck a pencil up the other.

In his imagination, 'Pop-out' stood there stunned, looking like a weird insect with feelers, while everyone cheered in unison "Rostrun! Rostrun! Rostrun!" Vic clasped his hands above his head in victory as 'Pop-out' sank to his knees in defeat.

Then, Vic snapped back into the gravity of the situation. Despite feeling fearful, the crazy image caused a snigger to bubble up from his stomach, and with dangerous speed it gurgled into his throat.

To laugh now would result in a fate worse than Rick Ward, so Vic bit the inside of his mouth hard and tasted blood.

Parsons, with stalks now receded, rotated on the spot, and eyed the whole class. He wagged his finger and hissed, "If Rostrun or any of you ever submit such an appalling assignment again, I will not be responsible for the consequences." Then he bellowed, "Class dismissed!"

Vic was last out and felt 'Pop-out's' frosty stare all the way to the door. Thank goodness it was the end of school for the week and also the start of the half-term holiday.

As he walked home Vic thought "I'll show him in the next project, I'll get a flipping fabulous mark - just you wait and see."

Little did he realise how true that statement would prove to be, and how amazingly that achievement would come to pass.

VR-B
The Family's Fortune

Most of Vic's journey home from school was on the flat. If he owned a bike, as most of his friends did, he would have been sitting down in front of the television in a few minutes. But, on foot, it took more like half an hour. However, on turning into Eden Lane, where he lived, the cyclist and pedestrian were on equal terms.

The hill was very steep. Only the fittest cyclists could get to the top without having to climb off with aching thighs. Even the world's greatest cyclists, used to gruelling ascents on the Tour de France, would be forced to stand up on their pedals and wiggle wildly from side to side to reach the top.

It wasn't much easier on foot.

Vic took a deep breath and began his ascent. To make the daily climb less tedious he often imagined he was a famous mountaineer scaling the snowy slopes of Mount Everest. On a good day, if no one was looking, he would even pretend to thrust a flag victoriously into the ground on reaching the summit.

However, today had been a particularly bad day. He found himself pacing like a soldier on a route march chanting quietly to himself, "I'll show Parsons! I'll show Parsons!"

He lived at number 42. Despite it being on the very crest of the hill it was not a house to be proud of. In fact, it would easily win the award for the "Worst kept property in the road", if there were such a competition. Due to the sheer embarrassment at its lack of upkeep, Vic preferred not to have friends over.

He carefully swung the gate open with both hands. The hinges were old, rusty, and ready to give way. It groaned loudly in disapproval.

The front door of number 42 was green, but not what you would call a posh green. Some colours catch the eye, but this one didn't - not unless you liked army colour schemes. On a decorator's paint chart among exciting colours such as "Vibrant Violet" and "Zesty Yellow", it could well be described as "Goose Poo". Having said that, there were flaky places, where the paint had peeled off, revealing a rich burgundy colour beneath. There was no doubt that the place had seen better days.

The house didn't have a name, unlike the two on either side. To the left was "Dellenellen"; a strange name Vic had always thought. That was where a quiet old couple called Derek and Ellen Dingle lived. The Dingles spent most of their time peeping through the crack in their net curtains, which shut in an instant if they sensed they were being observed. Vic was never sure whether they were nosey, or lonely, or perhaps both.

The house on the other side sounded really nice; "Cherry Blossoms". The residents there were noisy students from the local university. Goodness knows how many were packed in and the number seemed to vary daily, but they all seemed to know Vic and always said "Hi" to him. Number 42 just had two white plastic numbers nailed to the wall. And the number 4 was cracked and hanging at an angle.

There was a date in the brickwork of number 42 which said "1897". The large old-fashioned door knocker may well have been the original. There was an equally old letterbox with the word "Letters" cast into the metal flap. As he opened the door Vic thought, angrily, "What a stupid instruction! What else are you meant to push through ... knickers?"

"Hello", said a cheery but frail voice, "Is that you Vic?"

Nana always said that. But after the day he had just had it particularly annoyed him. Who on earth apart from him could it be? He replied in a loudish voice, but not quite loud enough for her to hear, "No, it is I, flipping Tutankhamen, King of the Pharaohs!"

It was the first name that came into his head, probably because of the picture he had pasted on his Egyptian history project folder. But a fat lot of good that had done! An E minus, he still couldn't quite believe it!

For the first time in an hour he smiled. What a shock it would be for Nana if he were Tutankhamen in dazzling robes. He giggled as he imagined what her face would look like if the Pharaoh had walked into number 42.

"Greetings Nana, it is I, Tutankhamen. I have come to ask you to knit woollen socks to be placed in a sacred burial casket in my pyramid." But as he swept majestically through the front room into the 'middle room' as Nana called it, where they lived, ate, and watched TV, Tutankhamen returned to Vic in an instant.

"It's mince beef for tea. Is that all right?" enquired Nana.

Mince beef! Vic let out an agonising sigh. It was not that there was anything particularly wrong with minced beef, and Nana was not a bad cook. In fact, her cakes were delicious. However, mince beef was on the menu at number 42 far too much for his liking - mince in watery gravy, with boiled potatoes and frozen peas. However, he knew they were quite poor, and that Nana was doing her very best, and she loved him.

He trudged upstairs to wash his hands before the familiar meal. After his bad day, it would have been nice to sit down to the kind of feast that would have been laid on for a Pharaoh, hand-fed by attentive servants.

Sadly, however, Vic did not have any such luxuries in life. In fact, things were tough for him, if not tragic.

He did not have any parents, or at least he didn't think he had any. He knew that he didn't have any other grandparents apart from Nana; they had long since died. The whereabouts of his parents was something of a mystery.

His mother and father, Alf, and Alice, were famous archaeologists who worked for the World Institute for Objects of Antiquity. He had many magazine and newspaper articles that documented their finds from around the globe.

Their international fame had soared as a result of discovering a number of significant objects. These included the Marriage Necklace of Queen Tittinarpah (circa 2000BC), the Goblets of Gulpe (circa 900BC) and the Masks of the Phueybaum Warriors (circa 1500BC).

While ordinary people may never have heard of such things, in archaeological circles they were as exciting as winning the lottery. Not only that, but they were worth far more.

Sadly, for the Rostrun family, none of the associated wealth of their finds came to them. The objects either became the property of the government of the country in which they were found, or, in rare cases, they were donated to the World Institute.

So, despite the fame, the Rostruns were far from well off.

The big question that everyone always asked Vic was, "What happened to your parents?" It wasn't something either he or Nana liked to talk about, but this was the story.

About five years previously, his mother and father had left on a six-month trip to Central America. The purpose of the visit was to try and find evidence of an extinct tribe called the Matapopafetal. They were part of the famous historical race known as the Maya.

Very little was known about them except that they lived on the banks of the River Fuddi. It was a remote river in the darkest rainforests in a place called Guatemala. Now, in case you don't know where Guatemala is, it lies on that thin bit of land (at least on an atlas) that joins North and South America.

It was believed that the Matapopafetal were highly skilled architects. They developed amazing cities that rose out of the jungle. They were also renowned craftsmen and women who cast molten gold into the most amazing things. Stories passed by word of mouth, from generation to generation, spoke of incredible gold statues encrusted with precious jewels.

Now, if you ever plan on trying to find the River Fuddi in an atlas or online, don't bother, it's far too small. In fact, part of the Rostrun's visit was to try and locate the source of the river. They aimed to do this using the knowledge of local people who still lived deep in the rainforest. Much of the area is still uncharted territory that appears as green jungle on even the most expensive, detailed maps.

It had been agreed that during his parents' search for the Matapopafetal, Vic would live with Nana Nellie in Eden Lane. Then, on their return he would move back in with mum and dad in their normal home. So, having waved goodbye at the airport Vic had expected to see his parents again within sixth months, hopefully with some rare gold artefacts. But that was the last Vic saw of them!

After a year or so, during which time their disappearance had been headline news in all the national newspapers, Vic and Nana had a visit. Two important individuals came to see them at number 42.

The first was Professor Norman Uralt MBE, the Director of the World Institute for Objects of Antiquity. He was accompanied by Chief Inspector Saddleback of the local police, not to mention a gang of reporters and photographers. They jostled and pressed their noses against the window once Uralt and Saddleback were inside.

Vic noted that the two men were like 'chalk and cheese'. Uralt resembled a tall stick insect wearing a dreadful green tweed suit and round wire rimmed glasses. Saddleback was short, plump, and rather sweaty, and didn't quite fit in his uniform. The belt around his waist strained on the last notch and looked fit to explode at any moment. Mind you, his shoes were amazingly shiny, and Vic could see a distorted image of the room reflected in the toecaps.

"Mrs Rostrun", Professor Uralt began, "This visit is neither easy for you, young Victor, or us. I'm afraid I have some difficult news. You will both be aware that searches have been taking place for months for Alf and Alice. Staff have been sent from the Institute and have worked with local trackers to try and locate them. To date, no trace has been found. However, a few weeks ago a rucksack belonging to your father was found by local villagers floating down the River Fuddi. It is with great sadness that we now must assume that your parents have died, possibly in some terrible accident. However, Victor, you must be brave and proud as they were great people and true pioneers."

Chief Inspector Saddleback held his cap over his heart and nodded throughout Uralt's speech. He then added "Master Rostrun, may I say on behalf of The Force how sorry we all are."

After turning down the offer of a cup of tea and one of Nana's home-made Fondant Fancies, even though Vic was sure that Saddleback had been staring at them, they left briskly. They pushed and shoved their way through the crowds that were pressing against the house. Vic then shut the door while the photographers' cameras flashed wildly.

It was a moment Vic would never forget. He and Nana sat in absolute silence for ten minutes. He felt tears burning in his eyes and he saw Nana swallowing hard. Then Nana said, "Let's have a cake, shall we?"

* * *

"Wash your hands love, tea's ready", Nana called from downstairs.

Vic woke with a start. He had been lying on his bed daydreaming about his parents, Professor Uralt, Chief Inspector Saddleback and that terrible day. For a moment he felt that he had been back there. He thought he could even taste the Fondant Fancy on his lips. He got up from his bed and on his way to the bathroom noticed a book on the floor called "The Child's First History Book - No. 8: The Egyptians", Published 1985.

'Pop-out' Parsons was right. His history project had been researched from a nursery book. Not only a nursery book, but a rubbishy second-hand one found in the charity shop where Nana was a volunteer.

He kicked it as hard as he could. It slid across the linoleum floor and disappeared under the bed.

"Good riddance", thought Vic.

As he washed his hands he stared in the basin and watched the lather swirling down the plughole. He imagined an exotic ocean where the water might one day end up.

He wished he could just as easily disappear somewhere too.

VR-C
The Charity Shop

When Vic got up on Saturday morning he was still thinking about the awful incident with 'Pop-out'. Even though he didn't tell lies, he had decided not to tell Nana about the E minus. At least not yet!

Nana was doing a great job trying to bring Vic up and she always encouraged him to do well at school. Vic had no doubts that she would be really disappointed that he had got such a terrible mark. Every parents' evening, she put on her coat and a ridiculous furry hat and made her way to the school to meet the teachers. With her fat arthritic ankles, it took her hours to walk there. But she wanted Vic to succeed in life, especially now that he had such difficult circumstances to deal with.

Now, every Saturday Vic made the slow trek into town with Nana to do volunteer duties at the local charity shop, Agnes Allsorts.

On the face of it, it may not appear to be the coolest thing for a young person to do. Most would prefer to visit the local skate park or even hang around with the menacing gangs of youths in the shopping centre. However, there were three very good reasons why Vic was happy to spend six hours each week at Agnes Allsorts. One reason was noble and the other two were more selfish!

About ten years ago, Nana had 'lost' Grandad Rostrun to cancer. He had died when Vic was a toddler, just at the time he was taking his first steps. Vic had wished he had known Grandad Albert. He sounded a very interesting and funny chap and Nana liked to tell stories about him.

His favourite one was about a day when there was a freak force eight gale. Grandad rushed into the garden to collect the washing before it all blew away. For a bit of fun, he put a pair of Nana's huge knickers on his head, which looked like a chef's hat. But, to his horror, as he walked back into the kitchen, the Vicar had just arrived.

The Rev. Saintley had popped round to discuss the flower arrangements for the Harvest Festival with Nana. He looked quite shocked but didn't say anything, so Grandad thought it best not to draw attention to himself.

He stood there for the whole time with the bloomers on his head. That one always made Nana cry with laughter, although sometimes Vic thought there were tears of sadness too.

Even though he was a kind and gentle man, Nana said that he was also very brave. He had served as a sergeant in the paratroop regiment for the army in a number of countries. At his funeral Nana had made sure his raspberry-coloured beret was placed on the top of the coffin. Apparently, a number of his chums who attended the funeral stood to attention and saluted as it went up the aisle.

When he had been on his tours of duty, he always brought back strange things for the family. That's where Nana reckoned Vic's dad had got his interest in other cultures and archaeology.

During the last months of his life, when he was very ill, Grandad stayed in St. Agnes Hospice. Vic had heard from all sorts of people that it was an amazing place. Nana said the nurses and staff did a fantastic job looking after him until sadly he 'passed', the term she always used about death. As well as all the wonderful care, she remembered how they gave him a drop of whiskey in his tea last thing at night, which he loved!

Since that time, Nana had been a regular volunteer at the hospice shop. She liked to help them raise money for other sick people like Grandad Albert.

She had worked all her life in the clothing industry. As a young woman she began as a seamstress making garments. But she was so good that she soon became a supervisor and later what was called a checker. That job was all about ensuring the quality of the things before they were packed to send to the shops.

So, now in her old age, Nana had gone full circle and was back sewing and mending the garments that came into Agnes Allsorts. Even though she now worked much slower, Ruby Ramsbottom, the manager, always commented that her quality was 'second to none'. She boasted to customers that old clothes looked like new once Nana had spent half an hour on them.

Even though Vic sometimes wished he could do other things on a Saturday morning, he had a good heart. He knew that helping others, by giving a few hours at Agnes Allsorts, was important.

Now, the reason for the 'Agnes' in the shop's name was obvious. The 'Allsorts' came from the vast array of goods that were donated and could be purchased there.

Vic's job was quite simple! People brought in all sorts of things they no longer wanted, mostly in bin bags. He then sorted the things so Ruby could decide where on the scale of 'throw-keep-wash-display' the item should go.

Most Saturdays Vic got to sort a mix of clothes, books, ornaments, china, and what were termed 'miscellaneous' items. They could be anything and had their own separate display.

Having explained the worthy reason why Vic worked there, there were also two selfish reasons why Vic was happy to help.

Here's the first!

On Saturday mornings an eighteen-year-old girl called Jaz Ornery, really Jasmine, but she said she only got called that when she was in big trouble.

Jaz was a different sort of volunteer. She was doing a "Community Service Order". When Vic first found out, he thought that sounded very grand and quite an honour. It was only after a few weeks that Jaz explained that she had been caught stealing stuff from a shop in town, and not for the first time at that! She had ended up in court in front of a magistrate. 'The Beak', as she called him, had given her 150 hours community service volunteering as a punishment. It had been suggested that she used the hours to help a good cause. As a result, she had ended up working at Agnes Allsorts.

Jaz was a good ten years older than Vic. Even though he knew they would probably never get married, he really fancied her. She was just different to all the other girls he knew. She talked about all sorts of interesting things and loved motorbikes and Formula One racing, just like Vic. She had amazing spiky hair that regularly changed colour, cool clothes, and her perfume called 'Fairamoan', which he had spotted in her rucksack, smelt ace.

Vic often inhaled the heady scent that hung around her when they were bagging up the rubbishy old stuff to be thrown away, but never so loudly that she would hear.

The second selfish reason for working in the shop was due to the fact that he and Nana bought most of their clothes there. Ruby knew how hard things were for them. So, she kindly let them have the 'best pickings', as Nana called them, of anything that came in, that they liked.

The truth was that Vic didn't like any of those clothes. But he never said so to Nana. He knew she could never afford the expensive designer gear that most of his classmates had.

Very occasionally Agnes Allsorts had some good stuff. However, it was mostly used items from places like 'The Bargain Bazaar' or 'Tommy Thrifty' in the High Street. Those were the sort of places that most people walked past without even stopping for the merest window shop.

Anyway, Vic would never want to hurt Nana's feelings by making her think that she was not doing a good job looking after him. So, he made the best out of second-rate jeans and loud shirts.

Having said all that, on one occasion he had found some crumpled up money in the pocket of a pair of mustard-coloured trousers that she had chosen for him. The trousers went straight to the back of his wardrobe, but the cash kept him in secret sweets for over a month! So, from then on, he always made a careful search of all the gear that came in. Sadly, to date, there had only been that one find.

Well, that Saturday went much the same as all others. Vic sorted things in the storeroom with Jaz. Nana worked on the clothes. Ruby fussed around the customers saying how lovely they looked in an item of clothing, when actually they generally looked awful.

The only difference was that for once a box of books had been dropped off that were not old and out of date.

In the main, the box contained computing books on how to use various software packages. However, one particular title caught Vic's eye - 'Net Surfers'. It had a line of smaller text under the main heading that said, 'Advanced Wonders of the World Wide Web'.

Despite not having a computer, although his friends did, Vic knew quite a bit about the Internet. There was a computer club at school where, crammed three to a machine, you could get lunchtime access to pretty decent PCs. Most people played mindless games. Vic, however, was an information addict and loved doing research. Given the chance he could lose hours at a time finding out things most people would think of as irrelevant trivia.

That was why the E minus actually hurt his feelings more than 'Pop-out' realised. Projects like the last one on the Egyptians fascinated him. Given the chance, he would have come top of the class. The problem was how a budding researcher could manage with such poor resources?

The school library was adequate, in the online index you could find lots of titles, but someone always had the book you wanted. Normally, Brian Bane, the class bully, sprinted to the library whenever a project was set simply to deprive everyone else of the best books. No doubt he hid them rather than actually use them as his marks weren't that good.

The big public library in the town, for which Vic was the proud owner of a photo membership card, wasn't much better at providing what you wanted. Whilst the shelves were longer than the ones at school, the library served thousands of local residents!

Vic thumbed through the pages of 'Net Surfers'. It was fascinating. There were so many terms that he had never heard of, such as search engines, cookies, and artificial intelligence!

"This is a whole new world I never knew existed", Vic thought to himself. He knew about the Internet but had never really understood how it worked and it stirred his interest.

"Are you OK?" Jaz enquired.

"Sorry, what did you say?" replied Vic still studying the text. "Oh, yes I'm fine" he said, still engrossed. "I'm having a quick look at this book about the Internet."

"A quick look! You've had your head stuck in there for nearly half an hour!"

Vic looked up at the clock in the storeroom. It was true; he had been miles away thinking about computers and networks linked to each other around the world. At that very moment people were sharing information in places as far away as Chile and China.

It was then that he noticed that Jaz had just finished sorting a whole load of huge items of ladies' underwear.

"Looks like I found that book just in time" he thought to himself with some relief.

For a laugh, Jaz pulled on a pair of unbelievably massive blue knickers over her jeans. "Look at these whoppers!", she laughed. "There's enough room in these for you, Nana and Mrs Ramsbottom to join me. The owner of these must have had a bum the size of a bouncy castle! What do you think?" she said, posing like a catwalk model, pulling the waistband out at arm's length.

Vic paused for a moment.

Jaz sensed that even though he was giggling he wasn't really focussing on the mind-boggling bloomers but was lost somewhere in his own thoughts.

"I think" he said, "... that my life would be transformed if only I could get my own computer with global Internet access and networking. "The big question is how!"

VR-D
The Visit

Vic and Nana finished work early as Ruby Ramsbottom said she did not expect there to be a last-minute rush. Not that there ever was, as the staff normally outnumbered the customers!

Going home early was a double bonus as Ruby had said that Vic could have 'Net Surfers', which she noticed that he had been clutching for most of the day. She was pleased with how hard Vic had worked and didn't want him to go home unrewarded.

It was a good job that she had not seen the incident with the enormous knickers, especially as Vic had also tried them on and pretended to be Superman!

As they crept home at snail's pace, Vic was on the verge of starting a conversation a couple of times. He finally plucked up enough courage as they began to climb Everest.

"Nana, there is something I need to tell you and something I want to ask."

She invited him to speak with a nod as she was far too puffed out to talk.

"Well", Vic began, "I had a bit of bad news at school. Even though I tried really hard, I only got an E minus for my history project on the Egyptians", then without drawing breath he quickly added, "But it's all down to my research. If we could get a computer, I know I could get an A. You see everyone does Internet research at home these days, it's what you have to do!"

At this point he held up the new book triumphantly rather like someone who had won an international sporting trophy.

"So, can we buy one?"

Nana did not reply until they had got their coats off, they were sitting down, and she'd got her breath back.

"Vic, I know things haven't gone well at school recently, Mrs Fussington rang to check you were all right as they were concerned about your work. Now don't worry; I set her mind at rest and well done for being honest about the poor mark. But about a computer, even though your parents left you quite a bit of money when their house was sold, it's been put in what's called a 'trust'. Sadly, we can't spend any of it until you are 21. I know that seems crazy, but your mum and dad could never have imagined anything like this would have happened. I'm really sorry. It makes me sad to think of you missing out, but we just can't afford one."

Even though it was the answer that he had expected to hear, Vic's face dropped. It wasn't the first time he heard about his coming inheritance, but being 21 was a long, long way off and it didn't help him at all at the moment.

"However", Nana said with a ring of hope in her voice, "Collingwood rang yesterday to say he is flying in on business and will be staying with us as usual. Maybe he can come up with an idea; you know what he's like!"

Vic knew exactly what she meant. Things happened when he was around!

Uncle Collingwood was Vic's mum's brother and after her disappearance he did what he could to help him and Nana. The only problem was that he lived in Austin, Texas in the USA, which meant that his visits were limited to couple a year.

He was an immense man in every way, his size, volume, moustache, dress sense and, most notably, food consumption.

Thankfully when he came to visit, he treated Vic and Nana to meals out including breakfasts. Goodness knows how he would have managed on the mince rations.

Another immense thing about Collingwood (as everyone called him, even Vic) was his unbelievable consumption of Cola. It was the only thing that he ever drank, even at bedtime.

Whenever he came to stay, Nana had to buy in huge supplies, which Vic had to haul up the hill. He had often thought it might have been easier to have it delivered by tanker and transferred into the bath through a huge hose. Collingwood could then dip his glass in rather like you would when filling your glass from a bowl of fruit punch.

When they ate out, Collingwood always complained that the glasses were like 'Texan thimbles'. So, he chose to quaff from a bucket-sized mug, which he carried in the cavernous pocket of his enormous overcoat. Then, when seated in a restaurant he would present the bucket-sized mug to the waiter and say in a loud voice "Now fill that beauty, and don't you go light on the rocks" meaning a monster drink with plenty of ice. It was very embarrassing and made Vic cringe.

It must be said that for all his good points Collingwood didn't have great manners. In fact, he often farted violently regardless of who was in the room! On one occasion he even managed to string enough 'biffies', as he called them, together to play a tune of surprisingly varied notes although he did have to sprint for the toilet at the end of the recital.

However, of all the immense characteristics that Collingwood had, the one that everyone always remarked upon was his generosity. He always helped others.

On Wednesday of the half-term holiday, there was a deafening rap on the old knocker of number 42, so hard, that it was amazing it did not fall off.

Vic ran to open the door knowing it had to be Collingwood, and it was!

"VR my boy, how are you?" He always called Vic by his initials. Vic didn't mind in fact he thought it was cool!

"My, you haven't grown much!", which was always the second thing he said.

As he bent over to pick up his bag Vic could not help but notice his vast backside. "Sorry I can't say the same about you" Vic thought.

"Right then", panted Collingwood breathlessly, "Aren't you going to offer your old uncle a drink, especially as I've had to lug so many boxes out of the taxi?"

"Boxes? What boxes?" Vic enquired.

"That load!" laughed Collingwood pointing at the front garden. "Oh, and by the way, the gate came clean off the hinges as I was bringing them through, but it looks like you could do with a new one anyway!"

Vic peered into the garden and immediately guessed what it was – "Yes!" he cried, "YES! A computer!"

It took quite a bit of effort to get the boxes inside, not to mention about a litre of cola for uncle.

Pretending to be a warehouse manager, Vic stood at the door and checked the boxes as they came through. 'Keyboard' (check), 'Printer' (check), 'Scanner' (check), 'Cables & Accessories' (check), 'Monitor' (check), 'Router' (check) and finally the biggest box marked 'CPU floor tower' (check)!

The latter seemed by far the heaviest and caused Collingwood to fart a couple of times as he wrestled it in. "I hope you marked those two deliveries down as well?" winked Collingwood, referring to the smelly biffie blasts. Vic nodded and giggled.

So, there it was, Vic had a brand-new computer. Not only a computer, but the very latest top-spec gaming computer.

Whilst Collingwood had bought him some great things in the past, he had certainly come up trumps this time.

Collingwood mopped his brow with a large red checked handkerchief that looked big enough to be used as a tablecloth. "Right VR" he said, "Now the fun bit … getting this lot to talk to each other."

Vic opened the boxes whilst his uncle snapped off the polystyrene packaging. Within seconds it looked like it had been snowing in the front room as there were tiny white beads everywhere!

While Collingwood assembled the various parts on the table near the telephone socket, where he informed Vic the system router would need to be plugged in to get him online, Vic pretended to make a snowball with the bits of polystyrene. They were sticky with static! As fast as he flicked a bead off one finger it seemed to jump onto another. In the end Vic got so frustrated that he flapped his hands wildly to shake them clean.

Collingwood looked up. "Now quit fooling around you chump and come over here cos you're gonna need to know what goes where."

In the next half an hour, Vic practiced putting all the cables in the right places before booting up the computer.

Nana came in with some refreshments; a glass of milk for Vic and you can guess what Collingwood had. As she set the tray down, they were just discussing the wireless mouse.

"A mouse!" she squealed pulling up her skirt above her knees. In all the years Vic had lived at number 42, he had never seen Nana's knees before. But there for all to see were her legs, fat and very veiny. They looked a bit like a map of the London Underground, with blue, red, and purple lines criss-crossing everywhere.

"Collingwood, have we really got a mouse?" she cried.

"You sure have!" laughed Uncle, winking at Vic. "Go on, show her the critter!"

Vic obliged and held up the computer mouse. She screamed and beat a retreat into the kitchen followed closely by Collingwood trying desperately to explain!

He came back a few minutes later with a big grin on his face. "She sees the funny side now she understands, but she took some convincing before she would climb down from the chair!"

Then, in a more serious tone he said, "Now, promise me VR that you won't let this computer cause any falling out between you and Nana. She rang me up specially to see if I could get one for you, which I was delighted to do, but I don't want her to regret asking."

"I promise!" agreed Vic.

"OK, but here the three ground rules" advised Collingwood and he counted the points out in a military style:

"1. No messing with the kit, it's not a toy. 2. Even though I'll pay for the monthly hi-speed fibre-optic broadband connection, only short sessions on the Internet, and 3. Keep off those "chat rooms" you mentioned some kids at school use - there are some right weirdoes on them! Agreed?"

He thrust out a huge hand so as to shake on the deal. Vic willingly agreed and shook the clammy palm. Collingwood's fingers felt like fat warm uncooked sausages.

"Now when Texans shake on a deal, it's done, so don't you forget!"

Next, Collingwood showed Vic how to use all the computer hardware. Vic found the scanner particularly amazing. Turning pictures into digital images was unbelievable. Collingwood took a school photo of Vic from the mantelpiece and scanned it in. Vic watched as his toothy grin appeared on screen; it was a bit spooky to look at a digital version of himself on the computer.

"There you go, Vic Rostrun in virtual reality! VR in VR!" he laughed.

Collingwood split the following few days between meeting business clients and helping Vic. When he was not around, Vic spent most of his time with his head buried in his 'Net Surfers' book, increasing his knowledge of the Internet way beyond his mates.

On the last Sunday evening of his visit Collingwood treated Nana and Vic to the best steak meal with a mound of potato wedges at

Lou's American Diner. As they returned home, Vic turned to Collingwood and said, "Thanks for everything, you're ace!"

Collingwood's eyes seemed a little watery. "You deserve it all", he replied and patted Vic on the back.

That night, Vic couldn't sleep. It was all too exciting!

Even though he felt sad that Collingwood was leaving the next morning and it was time to go back to school, the past few days had been the best he could remember. The future seemed much better now that he was set up with his own top of the range gaming computer.

In the dead of night, when the house was quiet, and Nana and Collingwood were both snoring like warthogs, Vic crept downstairs for another look at the computer.

He wiggled the mouse, and the PC woke up and his picture appeared on the screen.

"VR in VR!" He remembered what Collingwood had said.

He gazed at himself. Somehow, he just couldn't get the throw away comment out of his head.

VR-E

The Storm

When Vic woke up next morning, Collingwood had long since gone. He had to catch the 6.30am flight back to Texas and Nana said he had left the house around 3.00am. It couldn't have been that long after Vic had finally fallen asleep as his mind had been buzzing about the Internet.

But, on the table with the breakfast things, carefully laid out as always by Nana the night before, there was an envelope left by Collingwood. As Vic munched some cereal, he read the note:

> *VR,*
>
> *Sorry to have dashed off this morning without saying goodbye. I came into your room in case you were awake, but you were sound asleep - muttering something about cookies. I guess you must have been hungry in your sleep! Anyway, I hope you enjoy the computer – and no excuses for poor school marks now! Oh, and remember the deal! I'll try and pop back soon and you can impress me with your Internet skills.*
>
> *Best regards,*
>
> > *Collingwood.*

The walk to school on the first day back after the half-term holidays was always a slow one! A few nice days off always reminded Vic how much he disliked school – or at least some of it. For the first time in a week he remembered the incident with 'Pop-out' Parsons and as he approached Alderman Roberts School it didn't help his frame of mind to see that 'Pop-out' was on gate duty.

Whilst most teachers stood and daydreamed as the pupils filed through, 'Pop-out' used gate duty as an opportunity for a military inspection of the troops. And woe betide anyone that turned up in non-school uniform.

As Vic neared the gate, he could see that 'Pop-out's' attention was focussed on a boy named Robinson. "Look at your tie you miserable oik!" Parson screamed, "The knot is much too fat, and the tail is far too short - you know the rules. Sort it out now, laddie!" While Robinson untied the tie, 'Pop-out' withdrew a ruler from his jacket pocket to perform a quality-control check.

Vic crept past unnoticed.

It proved to be an ordinary day with the only highlight, if you could call it that, being a new science project on mushrooms and toadstools.

Miss Frale, the spindly science teacher showed an amazing time-delay film that speeded up the life cycle of fungi. In the space of a few seconds the soil erupted, and weird looking mushrooms sprouted into life, opened like umbrellas and then just as quickly as they had grown, melted into a disgusting goo. It was quite freaky and could have been part of a science-fiction horror movie.

As ever, Miss Frale battled to maintain control of the class. Most of the time pupils were shouting out things like "gross" and pretending to be sick, and the moment her back was turned a few threw wet chewed up paper pellets at the screen. Even though it was quite funny, Vic felt sorry for Miss Frale. She always tried hard to provide interesting lessons, unlike some teachers who just made them copy from textbooks, but her attempts were always sabotaged.

Once the film was finished, she switched the lights back on. "OK class" she warbled, trying to be heard above the din, "Your project is to write a report on fungi with some illustrations, and ..."

Before she could finish the bell rang and the class dismissed itself. As a stream of bodies tried to squeeze through the door, Miss Frale, still trying to explain the homework, got swept into the corridor waving helplessly.

Brian Bane, the class bully, used the diversion to pick on Vic and he shoved him really hard in the back. Vic lost his balance and hit the floor with a smack. Bane looked down on him and put a foot on his chest. "Bet you get an E minus for this project too, you stupid loser", he sneered.

Vic rolled over and watched him sprint off towards the library, scattering the class in his wake, determined to claim every book on fungi. He got up and brushed himself down. Despite the humiliation at the hands of Bane he actually felt fine. "There are going to be quite a few surprises on this project", he chuckled to himself.

The walk home was much brisker than the journey to school. The skies looked heavy, and the temperature had dropped. The wind was picking up and towering grey clouds swirled in the sky. It was about to rain.

Vic was still a fair way from Eden Lane when large warm raindrops, the size of the peas he would be having for tea, began to fall. At first, Vic could count them as they spattered on the pavement. Then, within a minute, the heavens opened, and he could hardly see where he was going. It was the kind of rain that roared as it hit the ground, went back up and came down again!

In seconds he was soaked to the skin and even though it made little difference, Vic ran. He battled up the hill against the tide of water that was rushing down the pavement in rivulets. By the time he reached number 42 his heart was thumping, and he felt quite sick. He was grateful that the gate was lying on the ground, as it helped him to get into the house even quicker.

"Is that you, Vic?"

He stood on the doormat with raindrops dripping off the end of his nose. Even if he had wanted to be cheeky, he couldn't. It took him a good minute to get his breath back.

Nana came through and made the 'stutting' noise that she always used to show her disapproval. "You're wet through! Get those sodden clothes off now."

Vic moved to go upstairs to his room, but Nana had other plans. To his horror she made him strip down to his pants by the front door. Even they were wet, but thankfully he was allowed to keep them on.

Nana gathered up his steaming clothes. "Now go on 'knobbly knees' and get some dry clothes", she directed. Vic smiled; the comment about his unattractive legs was rather ironic after the mouse incident the other day!

When he came downstairs, Nana had put some warm milk and one of her delicious homemade shortbreads on a tray. He took them into the front room.

Even though it was daytime it was almost dark, and Vic had to turn the light on to see what he was doing. He took a peep out of the window. The stormy sky was incredible. It was an eerie pale green and the streetlights had come on early.

He settled down with his refreshments and switched on the computer so that he could do some science research on mushrooms.

Using one of the 'search engines' that he had read about in 'Net Surfers', he created a search on mushrooms. The computer thought for a mere second while information was gathered from around the globe. Vic found this bit utterly amazing. Then, he was presented with masses of 'hits' of websites with fantastic fungi facts.

Within an hour, Vic had more than enough information and pictures to copy into the word processor to create a great project. The text would need a bit of editing, but it was great not to have to start writing from scratch and by hand.

He even found a link to a joke website that had a mushroom and toadstool section. It was bizarre how the Internet could come up with such creative connections. He decided he would add a few puns on certain pages to liven things up as Miss Frale often seemed so sad.

He stood up in front of the computer and for a bit of fun read them out loud, imagining he was a famous comedian on stage.

"Ladies and gentlemen, why did the mushroom always get invited to parties? (Pause while the imaginary crowd looked puzzled) Because he was such a fun guy … get it? Fungi!" The crowd roared.

"Why did the toadstool get off the bus? Because there was not mushroom inside … much room." By now, in his daydream, Vic's make-believe audience were crying with laughter. One man had even fallen off his chair and was rolling around helplessly on the floor.

"And, to close the show", said Vic, "Why did the fungi family never go on holiday? Because it was spore … get it? Poor."

By this time the crowd were beside themselves and Vic imagined finishing his routine to a nice drum roll.

"BOOM!"

As Vic finished his play-acting with a bow, Nana came running into the room, her face as white as a sheet. She didn't seem to notice he was messing around, and warbled, "Vic, I'm just going to sit somewhere quiet, you know how petrified I am of storms!"

It was then that Vic realised the loud drumbeat in his daydream had actually been a massive clap of thunder outside. The timing had been uncanny!

He peered out of the window again.

"Phew" he whistled. The sky was now an even weirder colour – a swirling mass of deep purple and mustard. Within in an instant a fork of bright pink lightning cracked to earth behind the houses opposite, with another deafening boom. There was no gap between the lightning and thunder, which meant the vicious storm was directly overhead.

Normally, Vic didn't mind storms but the ferocity of this one made him shiver! He had never seen anything like it.

He ran through to check Nana was OK. She was nowhere to be seen! Then, Vic noticed the door to the cupboard under the stairs was open just a crack and one startled eye was peering out!

"Are you all right Vic?" wobbled a voice from within. The question would have been better asked the other way around.

Vic opened the door and there was Nana sitting on a small pouffe, as she called it, amongst the mops and brooms. There was another massive crack of thunder, which shook the house. The cupboard door slammed shut.

Vic ran back into the front room to check the storm. Just then, as he was passing the computer, the most incredible thing happened. The house was hit by lightning.

There was another huge boom, but this time there was a blinding flash of light in the room. Vic's hair actually stood on end.

An instant after the flash, Vic jumped out of his skin. All the wires on the computer were alive with bright blue electrical energy. It sizzled like sausages, dancing back and forth along the cables.

It snaked around the computer like mini bolts of lightning. Then, suddenly, as if all the bolts were communicating with each other, they joined as one and slowly moved towards the scanner.

For what must have been only seconds, but which seemed like minutes, Vic watched the blue electricity crackling around the lid of the scanner until, with a shrill whistle and a pop, it disappeared.

"Wowser!", Vic whispered.

He ran through to check that Nana was all right and a voice that came from the downstairs toilet confirmed she was. "We must have had a direct hit", warbled the voice. "I hope everything is OK."

Vic bounded upstairs to check there was no damage or, even worse, a fire, but all was well. The only thing that seemed to have been affected by the lightning strike was the computer. He chased back downstairs, fearing it may be ruined.

On first impression it was fine, although the mouse felt hot. The only weird thing was the screen. Vic stared at it with amazement. No, he was not imagining it; a brand-new icon had appeared. It was a vivid blue dot, pulsating from a pale shade to a dark one and back.

Vic moved the cursor over it and there was a faint crackling sound. Underneath the icon, it mysteriously said 'Guardian'.

VR-F
The Sprite

When Nana came into the front room, Vic was gazing at the pulsating Guardian icon with an astonished look on his face.

"You look a bit frightened love", she said, "And I'm not surprised after that lightning strike. It smells a bit funny in here, is that computer of yours, OK?"

"Yes, I think its fine. The screen just went a bit funny".

Vic didn't dare tell her about the crackling blue energy that had danced all over the PC, for fear of worrying her. If she suspected anything was up with the computer, the chances were that she may not let him use it. And there was no point mentioning the Guardian icon. For one thing, she had no idea what an icon was and, besides, Vic had no idea what it did. So, he thought it wiser to say nothing until he had investigated it.

"Right", said Nana, "After all that excitement it's time to switch that thing off and have tea. I expect after all that fast food you'll be glad to have some home cooked mince, potatoes and peas."

As Vic shut the computer down, he had a vision of the scrumptious burger he had enjoyed the other day. When he compared the two options, it was amazing that the same meat could be presented in such different ways, but there was no doubt which variety he preferred.

He also remembered the deal he had made with Collingwood, so he didn't try and argue with Nana for more time on the PC, even though he was desperate to click on the shimmering blue dot.

Throughout the meal, while he had a bath and was getting ready for bed, the only thing on Vic's mind was the curious icon. Guardian, what on earth was it? Perhaps it was some software that Collingwood had loaded, and the burst of electricity had simply caused an icon to appear. It was the only idea he could come up with. But, whatever the case, it needed investigating and he had formed a plan.

There was no way that he could bear to wait until tomorrow to check it out - he simply had to double click on the icon as soon as possible. So, as he settled down in bed, he set his smartphone alarm to wake him at midnight, which was much quieter than his bedside clock which went off like an alarm at a fire station. Vic knew by that time Nana would be snoring, and he would have the opportunity to check out, undisturbed, whatever Guardian was.

The hours until midnight passed so slowly. It was infuriating. Vic lay and watched the hands on his bedside clock. Even though he could hear the clock ticking, they hardly seemed to move. Ten o' clock. Quarter past ten, then half past. A quarter to eleven. It was an agonising wait. Then, at eleven o' clock, he heard Nana padding upstairs whistling quietly to herself, which she often did, and her bedroom door click shut.

Vic got out of bed, opened his door, and spied out. Sure enough there was a thin strip of light beneath her door. Then, after what seemed like an age it suddenly went black. Vic pressed the button on his smartphone. The face lit up - 23:10.

He needed to give her time to settle, so he tiptoed back to his room and lay on his bed. He shut his eyes and pictured the image of the blue icon, and his imagination began to run wild.

Suddenly, he woke with a start to the sound of his phone beeping. For a moment he lost his bearings, but then after a shake of his head, he realised where he was. "Gracious", he thought, "I must have dozed off". He got up for the second time and this time crept out onto the landing and pressed his ear to Nana's bedroom door. There were rhythmic snores coming from inside - a slight piglet-like snort followed by what sounded like "fissssssshhhh". Then there was a mutter: "Eight slices of your best ham please." Vic thought "Great stuff, she's snoring and dreaming."

The coast was now clear.

He sneaked downstairs, taking particular care not to put too much weight on the creaky third stair from the top, which always complained when you stood on it.

As he sat down in front of the computer, the only noises he could hear were the old fridge whirring in the kitchen and his heart thumping in anticipation of what he was about to discover.

He wiggled the mouse and the sleeping screen flickered into life. The toothy grin on his school picture was instantly displayed and it lit the room with a pale light. Vic checked the computer desktop and breathed a sigh of relief. He had half expected the Guardian icon to have gone and had seriously wondered whether the whole thing had been a daydream. But, to his relief, it was still there, shimmering in a hypnotic way. As he moved the cursor over the dot it crackled like dry twigs being thrown onto a fire.

Vic took a couple of deep breaths and with a shaking hand on the mouse, double-clicked on the icon as you would to launch any other application.

Nothing could have prepared him for what happened.

In an instant the screen transformed from the flat two-dimensional image of his photograph into an amazing three-dimensional view. The screen was light purple around the edge graduating to a deep indigo colour at the centre. Then, one by one, blue rectangles appeared at various points around the edge of the screen, which zoomed away, converging on a single point at the centre. There was no doubt, he was looking down a tunnel.

He screwed his eyes up and focussed on the darkest spot at the centre of the screen. He thought to himself, "I wonder how far it goes and what is at the end, if there is an end."

But before he had any more time to think, something else grabbed his attention. For a split second he was sure he had heard something. Yes, there it was again, a faint jangling noise. At first it had hardly been noticeable, but as he strained his ears, he could definitely hear something that sounded like someone gently shaking a set of keys. And, without doubt, the noise was getting louder.

Then, in the centre of the screen, a small silver dot appeared. It was increasing in size just as the sound was increasing in volume. Vic suddenly realised that something was coming down the tunnel.

His heart raced with anticipation. A part of him wanted to switch off the PC for fear of what might be about to happen, but he felt compelled to watch.

"Whoa", said Vic in astonishment, "It's a creature of some kind!" The thin arms and legs were now clearly visible and seemed to be waving as the 'thing' flew towards him. It was getting close now. Vic could see the limbs were covered in a criss-cross of thin glowing wires and pinpricks of light were chasing around its body. The head was quite small and was a perfect cube shape. It had bright blue features and unnaturally large ears that looked like two yoghurt pots glued on either side of the face. The creature was dressed in a metallic tunic rather like a suit of chain mail armour, and as it reached the end of the tunnel Vic held his breath in amazement.

As it stared at him, it moved its head back and forward, from side to side as though it were scanning Vic's features in micro-detail. It was deeply disconcerting!

Then, in a voice with a tone that sounded like knives and forks being dropped on a hard floor, the being spoke. "Greetings, Vic Rostrun, I am Spike Sprite the Portal Sentry assigned to your computer. I have been sent by the Guardian of Virtual Reality."

Vic managed a very quiet "Hi there", which did not sound half as grand, but it was the only thing that came into his head.

Spike Sprite continued.

"Portal Sentries lay dormant, deep in the circuitry of all computers and are only activated when rare and risky circumstances occur."

"Am I in danger?" Vic whispered anxiously.

"It's possible", said Spike Sprite "Although now that I have been activated the immediate crisis is over."

"Crisis?" Vic hissed alarmingly. It was all he could do not to raise his voice, but to wake Nana now would be a disaster.

Spike Sprite raised one of its slender hands as if to calm him.

"Wow" thought Vic to himself, "Only three fingers".

"Vic, I will try to explain to you in simple terms what has taken place, but even then, you are going to have to use your wildest imagination to accept it."

Imagination was not normally an issue for Vic but even he was struggling to take all this in.

Spike Sprite continued.

"If a huge blast of electricity, called a 'spike', surges through the circuits of a computer it can cause all sorts of damage. In some cases, it can even destroy it by frying all the chips and melting the motherboard. But perhaps even more dangerously, it can open a portal, a sort of door, into virtual reality. Once open, things can pass from your world into the digital world within the computer, in which I exist. Things can also travel the other way. This can have the most disastrous consequences."

Vic screwed his face up and thought for a moment. "So, was my computer spiked when the lightning struck the house? Is that what all that dancing blue energy was?"

"Not only was it a spike" the Sprite replied, "but it reached 9.15 mega-sizzles the largest ever recorded in our virtual databanks. It is astonishing that your PC wasn't destroyed! But as a result, the circuitry of your computer has been transformed and a bi-linear-digi-data-conduit, a sort of tunnel into the computer world, has been opened. As a necessary safety measure, I have been installed. You completed the activation when you clicked on the Guardian icon. The portal you can see behind me is the gateway to a virtual world."

For a moment Vic took his eyes off Spike Sprite and stared into the purple portal. He screwed his eyes up and focussed on the most distant point of the tunnel. It was weird. It seemed to be drawing him in, and it made him feel a bit giddy!

"So", said Spike Sprite "I am here to guard this portal and to make sure that if you choose to use it and enter the virtual computer world, you act sensibly and wisely."

Vic's chin nearly hit the floor. "Use the portal!", he exclaimed in a loud voice that could well have woken Nana; luckily, she kept snoring and mumbling about ham. Realising his error Vic continued quietly, "What do you mean, I'm allowed to pass back and forward into virtual reality in the computer?"

Spike Sprite looked surprised. "Why of course, you are the owner of the PC! You may use the portal whenever you like. But if you ever do anything that places you or anyone else in serious risk of injury or death, I shall return you and anyone else using the portal to safety and undertake a terminal system shutdown and the computer will become useless."

Vic could hardly take it all in.

VR in VR! Collingwood's words had come amazingly true.

A very quiet minute passed during which Vic paced round the front room, trying to grasp what Spike Sprite had explained.

Eventually, he spoke, "OK, so I can enter virtual reality, but how on earth do I do that?"

VR-G

The Spores

The light was so bright that Vic could see the veins showing through the skin of his hand. The glare around his fingers was too much to bear and as Vic blinked, he could see the shape of his palm on the back of his eyelids.

While Collingwood had told him to always use the scanner with the lid down, he was sure that given the bizarre circumstances there was no option but to do exactly what Spike Sprite had said. I mean, how often do you get instructions from a Portal Sentry?

The process for entering virtual reality on his modified PC seemed too simple to be believed.

Spike had begun by explaining the incredible virtual world that Vic could now enter.

"When you load up the Internet your web browser loads in the pages of information. You can read the text, look at the images, hear the sounds and watch the movies. All of that data exists in computer code. But, after a serious spike, that code is radically transformed. A precise copy of the things you can see on any website is created in a virtual world inside your PC. The places, objects, creatures and people are replicated as digital code in a secret processing chip."

Vic nodded as though he understood everything completely, even though he didn't.

"Now" continued Spike Sprite, "The bi-linear-digi-data-conduit, the purple tunnel you saw, enables you to enter this secret chip and the virtual world. You select your destination by having an image on screen chosen from your search engine browser, which you want to visit. You then click on the Guardian icon, place your hand on the scanner and hit the 'Scan' button. The computer scanner will sense your palm and know to mutate your human DNA into digital code, and your journey begins".

At this point Vic was completely baffled and asked a number of questions that began with "How", "Why" and "What"! But having done so he was still none the wiser so, perhaps foolishly, he agreed to have a go and see how it worked!

On the spur of the moment he couldn't think of where on earth to go, so he chose one of the recent Internet pages he had visited while doing his mushroom project for Miss Frale.

It was an amazing web site about an American bio-research company called Mushy-Tech Inc., which is involved in the genetic modification of fungi. They had cloned an ordinary edible mushroom with cells from the Sequoia Sempervirens, the largest tree in the world, and a species of bamboo that grows at around 90cm per day, the fastest growing plant in the world. The result was a massive mushroom that, given the right conditions, would sprout up within minutes.

It sounded a bit far-fetched but one picture on the website showed a scientist in a white coat straining to hold one of these super-mushrooms. It was a stupendous size; enough to provide a 'fry up' for a family of four. There was a daft caption underneath which said, "If you want mushrooms as big as heck, rely on the science of Mushy-Tech."

Well, it was on this site that Vic had found a fascinating picture of some spores. These are the special type of seeds that mushrooms spread, multiply and grow from. One of the images showed some mega-mushroom spores magnified under a microscope. At the time they had fascinated Vic, so he decided to display the picture in his search engine browser as his selected virtual destination.

It all seemed very bizarre. Here he was in the dead of night, in his front room, standing in his pyjamas, about to be transformed into digital code and destined to disappear into his PC.

As the scanner light moved under his hand, he wondered if it may have been worth popping upstairs to put some proper clothes on! I mean, was it wise to enter virtual reality without underwear? Nana would have definitely said "No" and would have expected clean ones at that! As she frequently reminded him, "You just never know what might happen". Anyway, it was too late now!

The scanner completed its scan of Vic's hand and the blinding light clicked off. For a moment, nothing happened. Vic pinched his leg with his free hand to check that this wasn't just one of those crazy dreams he often had, but it definitely wasn't.

But then something most certainly did happen.

Beginning at the tip of his toes he could feel 'pins and needles'. It was a bit like when you have been lying on your arm in the night and you wake up and it feels like it isn't there anymore. Then, as you move the limp limb, the feeling starts to come back, and you get the most agonising pins and needles feeling that is too much to bear.

Well, Vic was experiencing that same sort of discomfort, but now the sensation had left his feet and was moving up his body.

He took a quick peep at his feet and shrieked. To his horror they had been replaced by a shimmering mass of bright blue numbers. As he stared at the place that had been his feet a few seconds ago, he could now see a mass of tiny 0's that were frantically changing into 1's and then almost as quickly returning to 0's again.

"This must be my DNA changing into digital code", he concluded. "Totally wacky or what?"

Then his legs changed, swiftly followed by his waist. Vic could now sense the numbers whirling round his pyjama top and upwards towards his neck. As his head mutated, he heard a loud whooshing noise, and he entered the computer.

VR was in VR!

The first thing he noticed was that his body appeared to look normal again. The inside of the computer was boiling hot and within seconds, beads of sweat were pouring down his temples. He wiped his pyjama sleeve round his face and grinned at Spike, who was bobbing around next to him.

"Welcome inside your PC!" said the Sprite.

He held up his three-fingered hands and invited Vic to give him two 'hi-fives' or in this case two 'hi-five-threes'!

"This is how Portal Sentries greet each other", he instructed. As Vic's hands touched Spike Sprite's he felt a click as a small electric shock discharged into his fingers.

Over Spike's shoulder, he could see the view back into the front room through the computer monitor. It looked strange and distorted like the mirrors at a funfair that make you look weird.

"Well, are you ready to fly?" enquired the Sprite. Vic nodded and took a deep breath.

Without any warning he started moving at an alarming rate as they entered the tunnel. He could only imagine it must be what an astronaut feels as a rocket blasts off into space. He was flying not headfirst, but in a standing position, with his pyjamas flapping wildly in the force of the acceleration. It was better than any ride you could pay for at a theme park!

Vic could sense that Spike Sprite was right beside him although the speed was so great that he couldn't fully turn his head.

There was nothing for it but to simply enjoy the journey!

Suddenly, he landed with a thump and rolled over and over before coming to an undignified stop lying on his back, laughing. "That was amaaaaaaazing!", he yelled.

The Sprite ran over to him. "Don't worry", Spike laughed, "You'll get better at the landings with practice! Now, there is one more thing I need to explain before I leave you to explore – how to get back!"

Spike pointed behind them. There on the ground was a shimmering blue dot similar to the icon on his computer screen. The only difference was that this one was big enough to get both feet on.

"If you stand on there for five seconds you will travel back to your front room", instructed Spike. "As a Portal Sentry, I will always be here to meet you to check the portal is safe." And with that, Spike Sprite disappeared!

Vic looked around.

He was sitting on what appeared to be masses of thin grey stalks, about the length of your arm. He picked one up and waved it around like a sword. It was very light; in fact, his movements caused others to float up into the air.

It was as a few moved that he then realised he was standing on a floor of highly polished glass. As he looked up at some of the stalks floating above him, he noticed something else curious. It was a large silver tube with a glass dome on the end and it was pointing right at him. There were other tubes above him pointing out in different directions. It looked weird, but then again it was strangely familiar.

Vic sat down on the glass among the stalks to think.

"Eureka!" he cried out, "I'm sitting on a massive microscope and this glass is the slide, so these stalks have to be ..." He paused for a moment to think about what was on the computer screen before he entered virtual reality. "Of course, these stalks must be massive mushroom spores. The picture on the Internet was showing a close up shot of spores taken through a very high-power microscope."

Vic then drew breath as he realised something quite incredible. "These spores aren't massive", he thought, "I'm tiny! Somehow I've shrunk!"

He then heard a very loud bang and looked round. There coming towards the microscope was an enormous scientist, with an enormous ginger beard wearing an enormous white coat with Mushy-Tech Inc. embroidered on the breast pocket.

Before Vic could do anything, the scientist was peering down the microscope at the spores, and more importantly at him.

Vic froze.

He could see the pupil of the scientist's eye blinking on the lens above him.

Suddenly a voice boomed out, "What the! Jeepers! Randy, come and look at this. You won't believe it but there's a tiny kid in jim-jams sitting on the slide with the mega-spores!"

The door opened and boomed shut and another scientist who was obviously Randy, came over to take a look.

Vic didn't want to find out what would happen next and ran.

"Gee whizzer!" boomed Randy, "The little critter's running around. Quick Hal, pass me those tweezers!"

Vic sprinted for the shimmering blue dot at full speed, disturbing all the spores around him. They rose like a mist. As he jumped for the portal, the cloud was so dense that he had to swipe at the air to protect his eyes. But, thankfully, in the haze he managed to land on the dot.

He started counting. The scientist's tweezers began to move menacingly towards him across the glass slide. The points snapped like the jaws of a hungry crocodile. One, two, three (they almost got him), four, (they lurched towards him again) five!

Suddenly Spike Sprite appeared next to him, and Vic felt the pins and needles and whirling numbers sweeping up his body. In an instant he was zooming back down the purple tunnel with his heart pounding.

The next thing he knew, he was standing back in the front room with his hand on the scanner. "Man alive that was close" he panted, "Far too close for comfort!"

He looked at the computer screen where Spike was looking at him with a big blue smile on his cubed face.

"The first lesson in virtual travel", he laughed, "Everything is not what it seems! Normally you exist in VR as your normal size, but as you entered a highly magnified image you ended up getting shrunk. So, VR is not without its risks, however, it's also not without its benefits. Take a look in your hand."

Vic realised that one of his hands was clenched in a tight fist. As he uncurled his fingers, he saw some tiny whiskers in his palm.

He looked at Spike Sprite amazed and in a hushed voice said, "They're mushroom spores!"

Little did he know how vital these feathery flecks would be.

VR-H

The Institute

After the narrow escape at Mushy-Tech Inc., Vic felt quite wary about making another virtual visit. A vision of the huge tweezers clicking had woken him up in a cold sweat several times during the night, so he decided to have a few days off before journeying back inside the computer.

The following evening was the night before his science project had to be handed in, so he spent a far less exciting time putting the finishing touches to his folder. Having said that, it looked really good, and Vic was delighted with the finished article!

As well as information on different varieties, the folder had an impressive section on poisonous fungi and the terrible side-effects you could suffer if you ate one. In some cases, this included a gruesome death, so he had drawn a skull and cross bones in the margin next to those types. The project also had lots of colourful pictures that he had printed out from the Internet and of course there were the corny jokes.

But the highlight of the folder had to be his detailed explanation of how mushrooms spread and grew. To illustrate this, he had taken a few of the Mushy-Tech Inc. spores which he had presented under a piece of sticky tape. He was certain that no-one else would have managed to do this. Without doubt this had to be the best project he had ever handed in, and he was sure Miss Frale would be impressed.

And she was!

The following Friday the work was returned. It was nothing like as tense as when 'Pop-out' Parsons gave projects back. Miss Frale seemed resigned to allow wild cheering for those who had done well, and woeful jeering for those who hadn't.

After the majority had received their work back the process neared a conclusion.

"Bane", warbled Miss Frale weakly, "C minus. Not very good Brian". It was the worst mark so far and everyone made noises like braying donkeys. Bane fumed, returned to his desk, and slammed his folder down so hard that the pages flew everywhere.

At that moment there was a loud rap on the door and almost immediately it flew open so violently that it nearly came off its hinges. 'Pop-out' stormed in and within a millisecond you could have heard a pin drop.

"Miss Frale" began 'Pop-out' in a smarmy voice, "I was passing and wondered whether everything was all right? It sounded far too noisy for my liking."

He scowled at the trembling class.

"N, n, no, everything is f, f, f, fine" stuttered Miss Frale, looking as scared as her pupils. "I am just returning some w, w, work in fact, here's the l, l, last one, Vic Rostrun."

Vic couldn't believe his luck. Another project returned under the severe scrutiny of Parsons; how unlucky could you get. Everyone held their breath. Miss Frale checked the folder. "Yes, well done, an excellent piece of work - A plus!"

There was a stunned silence as Vic proudly walked up to collect his folder. As he passed Parsons, he could see his eyes bulging, not in anger, but in utter shock. He made the most of the moment and acted as though he were a famous actor collecting an Oscar. Sadly, it was inappropriate to make a speech thanking Collingwood for the computer and Mushy-Tech Inc. for the spores, so he settled for a slow walk back to his seat with a broad smile on his face.

When he got home, he proudly showed his achievement to Nana, and he was pleased at how much interest she showed in the folder.

"Did you get all this from the Instant-net?", she marvelled. "It's amazing what you can do on that CeePee. I saw you looking at those mushroom pictures the other day on the Voodoo-you, but I didn't realise you could print them."

Vic laughed! It was likely that Nana would never fully enter the 21st century and would be best sticking to baking cookies rather than generating them by visiting websites.

Now that it was the weekend, and Vic had a bit more time on his hands, he began thinking about another VR excursion. But where should he go? He would need to give it some careful thought, not wanting an experience like the last one!

It was during tea, as he mashed his potato in the watery mince gravy, that it came to him. It was such an inspiration that he almost said out loud, but thankfully he didn't, "I know, I'll visit the World Institute for Objects of Antiquity."

Vic had always fancied a visit where his mum and dad had worked. It was a great idea, I mean, what possible hassle could there be snooping around a crusty old museum after dark?

At 9 o' clock Nana said that she was going to make herself a 'hot toddy' and go to bed early as her ankles were giving her 'right old jip'. So, to the sound of various bottles chinking in the kitchen, Vic settled down to watch TV.

"Night love" said Nana as she shuffled upstairs, "Now, don't you stay up late watching stuff that'll give you bad dreams."

"You would not believe what has been giving me bad dreams recently" Vic chuckled to himself.

He knew that he would need to leave it at least an hour to be safe, so he settled down to watch something. He flicked back and forward over the channels but there wasn't much worth watching. The best thing was 'The Strongest Man in the Galaxy'. For the next hour, Vic watched gigantic oily-skinned men with bodies which looked like they had been inflated with foot pumps, lifting, and pulling immense objects. It was mindless stuff but then his mind was elsewhere.

Just before 10 o'clock a contestant called Ivor Grimhurnya who, as the manic TV presenter had mentioned at least ten times, was a descendent of the Vikings, was presented with a ridiculously large winner's trophy. Thankfully it signalled the end of the crazy contest and also a good moment for Vic to go and check whether the coast was clear.

He peered under Nana's door. It was dark and there was significant snoring. The 'hot toddy' had done the trick!

He tiptoed downstairs and fired up the computer.

The website for The World Institute for Objects of Antiquity didn't take long to find. As the home page loaded, Vic was greeted by a familiar image - The Masks of the Phueybaum Warriors. Underneath in small letters it said, "Discovered by Dr Alf and Dr Alice Rostrun."

Vic surfed the site, which was almost as boring as many of the items that the Institute had dug up.

There was a message from Professor Norman Uralt MBE, which explained that the work of the organisation was vital to all mankind. The eyes on his picture looked as uncaring as they did on that dreadful day at number 42, when he had brought the news about his parents. Nana had always taught Vic not to hate anyone, but Uralt, and 'Pop-out', stretched this to the limit.

Down the side of the home page were buttons marked 'Our Work', 'Our Research, 'Our Facilities' and 'Our Staff'.

Vic browsed the options.

His parents no longer appeared on the staff page, though there was a bit about a project to find the tribe of the Matapopafetal under 'Our Research'.

The facilities page proved to be the one that Vic was looking for. It had various pictures of the Institute - the outside of the imposing Gothic building, a huge library, museum rooms and finally a grand looking entrance hall.

"That" said Vic to himself, "Is where I shall start my tour."

So, with a picture of the hallway on the VDU, he activated the Guardian icon. Immediately, the screen transformed and in seconds Spike Sprite was zooming down the purple tunnel towards him. Vic felt no fear, just sheer excitement.

"Greetings Vic! I see you wish to travel to The World Institute for Objects of Antiquity, and I think I can guess why! Well, you know what to do."

Before placing his hand on the scanner, Vic checked his watch. 10.14pm. "I can't believe anyone is going to be there at this time on a Saturday night" he thought "So, here goes!"

It was just the same as before. The scanner's brilliance showed up the dirt under Vic's fingernails. Then there were the agonising pins and needles and whirling numbers that engulfed his body. And, before he could say 'bi-linear-digi-data-conduit', he was zooming down the tunnel with Spike beside him. The journey ended abruptly with Vic rolling across a highly polished floor.

Spike Sprite stood over Vic smiling. "I've placed the portal entrance behind that huge plant", he said, pointing to an enormous Aspidistra in the corner of the hall. Vic could see the bright blue dot pulsating behind the large terracotta pot in the gloom.

With that, Spike Sprite was off, and Vic got up and began exploring.

As well as having a majestic staircase that rose three flights, the hallway had a small exhibition. In fact, it was only the dim fluorescent lights in the display cabinets that lit the dark hall. Vic wandered around and viewed the contents: pottery, ancient weapons, part of a prehistoric cave painting and some brightly coloured Roman mosaics.

Where to next?

He took a look at the doors that led off the hall. Each had a neat hand-painted sign. Most sounded incredibly boring; 'Administration', 'Finance', 'Bursar' but one caught his eye: 'Professor N Uralt MBE'.

Vic tapped lightly on the door. Goodness knows what he would have said if anyone had opened it, but it seemed the right thing to do.

After a few seconds, he gently tried the handle. It was unlocked, and he crept inside.

The curtains were open, and a shaft of bright moonlight lit the room. But it was not enough for a proper look around, so Vic went over and clicked the desk lamp on.

It was exactly the sort of office you would imagine a Professor of Archaeology would have. It had old oak panels on the walls, leather chairs and it was disgustingly untidy.

There was a map on the wall with coloured dots showing the Institute's project sites around the world. Vic touched Central America. Whatever had happened, mum and dad were there somewhere.

It was then that his eyes fixed on Uralt's filing cabinet to the side of the map and, in particular, on a drawer marked 'Staff'.

The drawer squeaked in complaint as it opened. Within seconds he found the tab that said 'The Rostruns'. The file mostly contained boring paperwork like contracts, memos, and the odd crumpled note. But, tucked away behind the papers was something altogether more interesting. Vic recognised it at once – it was his dad's pocket diary! It must have been recovered in the rucksack that had been found, and Uralt had failed to hand it over.

He was about to take a look, but then stopped.

What was that? He was sure he had heard a noise. But he couldn't have; the place had to be deserted. Even so, he squeaked the drawer shut, but not before slipping the diary into his pocket.

There it was again! This time there was no mistake. There were footsteps and they were coming closer.

Vic dashed over and switched the lamp off but, in his haste, knocked over a half-finished mug of tea. The liquid spread out uncontrollably over the work on the desk.

The footsteps were now by the door. All Vic could do was to leave the mess and dive for cover behind a large leather settee.

The door opened, and the main light clicked on. Someone paced in.

Vic's heart was pounding so hard that he was convinced it could be heard.

The person went over to the desk and cursed. Vic heard the telephone being picked up and numbers being tapped.

"Hello, is that Security? Uralt here. Mr Knapper, could you come to my office immediately? There's been an intruder! ... No, I don't think they are still here, mind you I haven't checked. You're on your way, very good. ... Yes, bringing the guard dog would be sensible!"

The telephone receiver was replaced.

Vic was trapped!

VR-I

The Diary

There was a loud knock on Professor Uralt's office door.

"Come!" advised Uralt's voice. "Ah, Knapper my good man. Someone has been in here in the last hour. There's tea spilt all over the desk and as I am the only one on the premises apart from you, my only conclusion is that we must have a burglar!"

Vic lay absolutely motionless, hardly daring to breathe.

He could hear the guard dog pulling on a heavy chain lead and from the sound of its heavy panting it was just on the other side of the sofa. It growled a low menacing snarl as though it could sense the intruder was close by.

"Steady boy, steady", commanded Knapper.

Vic pressed his body against the back of the sofa trying to make himself as undetectable as possible. It smelt old and fishy, and he hoped the odour would disguise his scent.

"Well, sir, the blighter can't be in here, sir!" said Knapper, taking a quick look around. "In fact, sir, for some reason Fang got right frisky in the hallway near that big old plant sir. But I thought it best to make sure you were all right first sir, before checking elsewhere."

"Quite so!", replied Uralt. Then he said in a panic "The hallway! The display cabinets! I bet the scoundrel has broken in to steal one of the exhibits!"

With that, Uralt and Knapper, with Fang bounding at their side, rushed out to check the contents of the cabinets.

Vic knew he had to act fast. There was not a moment to lose as they would soon be back. He crept out from behind the sofa and tiptoed to the door. The search party had left it ajar, and Vic peered out into the hallway through the crack.

Uralt and Knapper, who Vic could now see was a short scrawny security guard in a blue uniform that looked like it hadn't been ironed for a year, were checking the Roman mosaic. Fang, an absolutely gigantic Alsatian dog that looked like it could well be the half-brother of a wolf, was prowling around their legs with his ears pricked up listening for the slightest sound.

Vic knew he had one chance to escape, and it was a slim one at that!

While their attention was on the exhibits, which were thankfully at the other end of the hall from the pulsating portal, he stepped out of the office.

With his back pressed against the oak-panelled wall, Vic tried his very best to blend in with the background, as a chameleon would. His drama teacher often criticised him by saying his acting performances in school plays looked 'wooden', but Vic hoped this was one occasion when this would truly be the case.

He edged his way towards the plant with his eyes fixed on the search party. It was probably only about ten paces to get to safety, but it felt like a kilometre. Bit by bit he crept towards the shimmering blue dot. It seemed to take forever.

"Well sir, all the exhibits seem intact" Vic heard Knapper report. "The robber must be elsewhere sir, or he's already made a clean pair of heels of it."

Vic was within one pace of the plant, and he made his move for the portal. It was as he lifted one of the branches to climb behind the Aspidistra that Fang sensed the movement and turned his head. His jet-black eyes focussed on Vic, and he barked the kind of bark that makes your hair stand on end.

He had been seen!

"There he is sir! The blighter is behind that big plant sir! Get him Fang!" And, with that Knapper fiddled with the chain and set the dog loose.

The Alsatian did not need a second command and bounded across the hall.

For a split-second Vic was paralysed with fear, but somehow managed to leap on the shimmering blue dot. He began to count. One, two, three, four - Vic could see two rows of white teeth as Fang leapt towards him.

When Uralt and Knapper caught up with Fang, they found him lying in a pile of soil from the upturned Aspidistra.

Knapper looked with astonishment at Uralt, who looked back flabbergasted.

"Where the heck did he go sir?"

* * *

Vic stood trembling; his sweaty hand seemingly stuck to the scanner. It took a number of deep breaths before he managed to peel it off.

Spike Sprite was looking out patiently from the screen of the VDU. "Well, that was another close shave. You can't say that your VR trips aren't eventful. I nearly had to shut the system down when you were about to be ravaged by that dog. However, that would have brought you back immediately without your dad's diary, which I know will be of great value to you."

"Thanks" said Vic as he felt the little book in his pocket. It was comforting to have something precious from his parents. He didn't have many such things.

"Oh well Spike, I'd better get to bed" Vic yawned. "It must be very late!"

He yawned so hard that his jaw clicked. It was definitely time for bed, whatever time it was.

He said goodbye to Spike and shut down the computer. As he wearily climbed the stairs, he clutched the little pocket diary. Even though he was desperate to read it, he just couldn't keep his eyes open. So, he tucked it under his pillow and promised himself a thorough investigation tomorrow.

*　*　*

"Hi Vic, how's things?" Jaz said cheerily. She was already sorting through her third bag as Vic walked through the door of Agnes Allsorts. "You look like you're half asleep!" joked Jaz.

The events at the Institute had taken their toll. Vic was exhausted! His eyes were puffy, and his face was pale. At breakfast, Nana said that he looked like he had had 'a night on the tiles', whatever that meant. So, he kept his head down as he crunched his cereal in case he looked guilty.

The morning seemed to drag, as there had not been much stuff left at the shop that needed sorting. Ruby Ramsbottom asked Vic and Jaz if they fancied having a go at some window dressing.

Vic looked shocked and immediately said "No thanks!". He had a vision of having to get undressed in the shop window and then putting on some terrible clothes while everyone in the street watched and laughed. Not only that, but the only underwear in his drawer that morning was a very old pair of large white Y-fronts, the sort that old men prefer. The thought of Jaz seeing him in those was unthinkable and would probably ruin any chance of a date with her for good!

Ruby seemed to read Vic's mind and quickly explained that window dressing meant creating a nice display. That actually sounded quite fun, and he and Jaz agreed.

Her idea was to have an 'orange' theme, which meant finding anything interesting of that colour to display. So, the best orange clothes, books and trinkets were chosen. Vic was actually enjoying himself kneeling in the shop window arranging things until there was a loud rap on the window.

A face was pressed hard against the glass. It was distorted and looked like a hideous gargoyle that looks down at you from a cathedral wall. Even so, Vic had no doubt who it was - Brian Bane!

He laughed and then pressed his open mouth on the window and blew out his cheeks in disgust at Vic. It left a sticky saliva smudge, which looked like a huge snail had been there.

At that moment Ruby came to see the display and spotted what was going on. She signalled in no uncertain terms for Bane to clear off. He responded with a very rude gesture that set Ruby off in a wild round of 'stutting'. She headed for the door to give Bane a good telling off, but he sprinted away, still gesturing above his head. Even though Vic was no friend or fan of Bane, he found it hard not to laugh at his nerve.

While Ruby furiously cleaned the smeary window, Vic and Jaz sat down in the storeroom for lunch.

It was while he was eating his peanut butter sandwiches that he suddenly remembered the diary in his pocket. He had completely forgotten it was there.

Jaz was reading a girl's magazine which Vic was hoping she might leave lying around. So, while hoping for a quick sneak at an article called '10 reasons to date a younger guy', which was featured on the front cover, he started looking at his dad's diary entries.

There was not a lot of interest from January to April, but in May, once they had flown out to Central America, things began to pick up.

May 16th - Canoed up the River Fuddi. Hot and sweaty. Hard going, especially as we reached the uncharted parts. Had to paddle the canoe and hack through branches and vines at the same time. Saw a snake as long as a bus!

May 17th - We had to leave the canoe – the river got too narrow and too many trees. Set up a temporary camp and went out on foot away from River Fuddi to look for signs of the Matapopafetal.

May 19th – Still no signs of tribe yet. Frustrating day walking around in circles in the jungle. Every tree looks the same.

May 20th – Eureka! Found an ancient hidden trail running beside the river. It must lead somewhere. We'll investigate tomorrow.

May 21st – Followed trail, pushed through trees, and found a huge clearing and ruins. Could be what we are looking for! Too dark to investigate. Went back to camp. Lots of snakes, some poisonous!

May 22nd - Searched the extensive city ruins. No signs of life or treasures. Strange carvings and symbols on walls – not seen these in any books. Found a large, sealed door – perhaps an entrance to underground passage? No obvious way to open. Strange discs with Mayan symbols by door. You can turn them and form different combinations. Perhaps there's a code to get in?

May 23rd - Researched and sketched symbols around ruins.

May 24th - More work on the Mayan symbols. Found five large sundials around the plateau, each with a different symbol on. Could these be the key to the coded dials?

May 25th - We have cracked the Mayan code. Alice, the genius, did it! We'll try the door tomorrow at first light.

From that date on, the diary was blank. Vic read the May entries three times before slowly shutting it.

"So, perhaps mum and dad did find the Matapopafetal", he thought to himself. "But then what happened?"

His imagination ran wild as he thought what might be behind the great stone door. Perhaps there was some fearsome wild beast, or maybe a flesh-eating dinosaur waiting to devour anyone who dared enter. Or perhaps the temple was a trap designed to capture anyone looking for secret treasure; once the door had shut you were imprisoned for eternity. Or perhaps behind the door was a slippery slope that carried you down to a lava lake at the centre of the earth.

Vic shuddered as he considered the possibilities.

But he had to believe that whatever was inside that temple it was still possible that his parents were alive.

It was then that he remembered something. It was something that may be very important. It was one of the crumpled pieces of paper in his parent's file in Professor Uralt's filing cabinet at the Institute. It must have also been found in his dad's rucksack with the diary. On first glance Vic had thought it was just rubbish, but now he clearly realised that the rough sketch of five circles with symbols was a vital piece of information.

Vic sat bolt upright and exclaimed, "I've got to go back and get it!"

Jaz looked up from her magazine. "Get what?"

VR-J

The Secret's Out

Vic stared at Jaz and realised what he had just said. Sometimes he wished he could keep his thoughts to himself. As much as he liked Jaz and she was probably his best mate, he was not sure he was ready to tell her about his strange computer. And goodness knows what she would think about his visits into virtual reality. It was hard enough for him to believe what was going on, let alone anyone else!

"Go back and get what?" asked Jaz again, intrigued as to what Vic was talking about.

He now had a very big decision to make; should he let his amazing secret out or not?

He was just about to tell a lie and say "I need to go back home and get a clean handkerchief" when his brain and mouth seemed to go into remote control. It was quite weird, almost like he was meant to tell Jaz.

He looked at her and in a quiet tone replied, "I've got to go back and get the piece of paper with the Matapopafetal code on from Professor Uralt's office at the World Institute for Objects of Antiquity".

Jaz giggled, "What on earth are you talking about? Have you bumped your head and gone nutty?"

Vic took a deep breath. "Jaz, if I tell you a secret, something almost too amazing to believe, something that's happened to me, would you promise to keep it?

Jaz looked concerned. "Vic, I'm not sure that keeping secrets is a good thing. Especially if you were to be in trouble, I'd have to tell someone else."

Vic thought for a moment and understood that what she had said made good sense. "OK" he replied, "No secrets, but if I tell you something that's going on will you agree not to tell anyone without discussing it with me first? Unless I'm in big trouble, then you can tell Nana."

"That's cool" agreed Jaz, "It's a deal". Vic held out his hand and made her shake on the agreement just like Collingwood had done with him.

He got up and peeped through the curtains that separated the storeroom from the main shop.

Ruby Ramsbottom was out at lunch and Nana was serving an old man at the till who was holding up a well-used garden spade. "They don't make 'em like this anymore, love!" he shouted. Nana told him the price. The old man tapped his hearing aid and shouted, "How much, love?"

As the conversation at the till got louder and louder, Vic pulled the storeroom curtains together as tightly as possible to give them some privacy. He then sat down next to Jaz so that he would not have to raise his voice as well.

Vic began to take Jaz through the whole story.

He started by explaining how he had got fascinated about the Internet after finding the copy of 'Net Surfers' at Agnes Allsorts. Jaz nodded and said that she remembered how he had had his head stuck in it for most of that day. Vic then went onto explain about Uncle Collingwood's visit. He described the amazing gift of the computer and how he had been learning to surf the Web.

He explained in vivid detail the incredible storm and the direct lightning strike on number 42. Jaz became more intrigued and as Vic described the blue energy and the strange Guardian icon that had mysteriously appeared on the screen, her mouth dropped open.

Outside, in the shop the bell went 'ding' to indicate that someone had come in. Vic, however, was too busy explaining things to Jaz, to notice.

He then told her about meeting Spike Sprite for the first time and did an amazing job explaining the bi-linear-digi-data-conduit and how it had opened up a way to travel through virtual reality to other places.

In the shop, the new customer could hear Vic talking quietly in the storeroom. They moved on from the second-hand bookshelves and hovered by the curtain.

"So" Vic went on "I then placed my hand on the scanner as Spike instructed and before I knew what was happening, my whole body was changed into a whirling mass of numbers. I disappeared into the computer and whizzed down this purple tunnel into virtual reality."

A single eye peered through the small gap in the curtains. Even though the customer's eye could not see much, the ears could hear everything!

Vic was now in full flow. "My first VR trip was amazing. I did some great research for my school project on fungi. I ended up walking on a massive microscope slide and collected some spores. As I was so tiny, the spores were as large as spears. Well, you wouldn't believe what happened next. These two scientists came into the lab and spotted me under the microscope. Then I nearly got caught by this giant pair of tweezers."

Jaz's eyes were now like saucers. The eye looking through the curtain was even bigger.

"I know this all sounds crazy, almost too crazy to be true, but honest Jaz, it's all happened."

Jaz sat silently, waiting for Vic to continue.

Vic was just about to explain about the visit to the Institute when he noticed a movement out of the corner of his eye.

"Hey" he shouted, "Who's there?"

The eye looked startled. Then, in a state of surprise at being noticed, a body stumbled into the storeroom tearing down one of the curtains as it fell.

It was Brian Bane!

He crashed onto the floor. Then in an attempt to get up, rolled around and became completely tangled in the cloth.

Before Vic could say a word, Bane, now looking like an Egyptian mummy, struggled up. As best as he could, he ran, though it was more like a fast shuffle, into the shop with the curtain wrapped around him. He pushed past Nana who whirled round like a spinning top. Then he bumped into a display of saucepans, which crashed to the ground.

Vic, Jaz, and Nana watched as the mummy fought its way out through the door and into the street. Bane part bounced; part bounded for a good hundred metres before daring to look back. Eventually he collapsed into an alley and breathed a huge sigh of relief that he'd got away.

"So, Rostrun reckons he's got a way of entering virtual reality" panted Bane to himself. "Now I've seen that in sci-fi movies; but in real life, nah ... he's got to be either the biggest liar, loopy or ..."

He stopped and then after a few moments said under his breath "Well, an amazing computer would explain the incredible turn around in his homework, especially that A in his science project. Virtual reality, well I never, it could just be true. Either way, I'm going to have to investigate more. Then, whatever the outcome, I'll sort him out once and for all!"

He kicked away the curtain that was still twisted around one of his legs and sloped off to devise an evil plan.

* * *

Back at the shop, the pots and pans were back in place and Nana was sitting on a chair in the storeroom. Ruby Ramsbottom had arrived back just after the commotion and was making a cup of sweet tea for all the victims. "If that Bane lad ever sets foot inside this shop again, it really will be curtains for him" she said angrily.

Vic looked at Jaz. "I think we had better finish our conversation later. That's if you want to hear the rest."

"Are you kidding Vic?" she replied, "You can't just give me half the story even if you are pulling my leg."

She saw Vic's face drop at her disbelief. "OK" she continued, "How about I come over later after work. You can then tell me the whole deal and show me the computer?"

Vic looked pleased and nodded.

He went through to check Nana was OK. She was sipping a cup of tea with one hand and fanning her face with Jaz's magazine with the other. He really hoped she hadn't opened it and read any of the articles. Some were about teenage love and totally unsuitable for Grandparents.

"Nana, would it be OK for Jaz to come over later?" Vic enquired. "She'd like to have a go on the computer?"

"Yes dear" Nana replied, "That's fine. I don't know why you don't have more friends over."

Vic reported back to Jaz. "Come over around 7.00pm". She nodded and they both got on sorting a few more bags of stuff before the shop shut.

*　*　*

At about 7.45pm there was a loud rap on the door of 42 Eden Lane. When Vic answered there was Jaz, smiling, with a big bottle of cola and a huge bag of popcorn.

"Some refreshments for the journey!" she said with a wink.

Vic took them. As they were about to spend the evening on the computer, it seemed quite fitting to have Collingwood-style refreshments.

Vic went through to the kitchen to get some glasses, closely followed by Jaz. Nana was sitting in her favourite chair, the one that used to be Grandad Rostrun's, watching her favourite soap opera.

"Hi, Mrs Rostrun" said Jaz, "How are you feeling after the antics at the shop?"

Nana looked up from her programme. "Oh, I'm fine thanks dear, although my ankles are a bit swollen. I guess you've come around to have a look at Vic's new CeePee; he's getting to be a real whizz on it."

Vic smiled. She didn't have the first clue about computers or, come to that, any technology. She would have not been at all surprised if Vic told her that he and Jaz needed to get changed into swimming gear before 'surfing' the net.

Vic poured the cola while Jaz tipped the popcorn in the largest glass bowl she could find, the huge one that was only used once a year at Christmas for Nana's sherry trifle. Even so, it spilled over the edge, and they had to eat a few handfuls just to tidy up.

The popcorn looked very grand in 'cut glass' and as they went through to the front room, Nana joked that it must be how Royalty ate theirs.

As they sat down to more handfuls of popcorn, Vic booted up the computer and then continued the explanation that had been so rudely interrupted earlier.

After a quick recap, he pointed out the Guardian icon which Jaz could clearly see shimmering on the screen. Then he got to the bit about his visit to the Institute to find out more about his parents.

Jaz looked intently at Vic as he described the diary, he had found in Uralt's filing cabinet, the frenzied search for him, and ferocious Fang.

As undeniable proof, he opened his dad's diary at the month of May and handed it to Jaz.

She spent a few minutes going through it, reading each day's entry aloud. As she recounted the Rostruns' progress Vic fired up the Internet in preparation for a search. Even though he was concentrating on the screen, he precisely mouthed the diary information as Jaz read it out. He had studied it at least a hundred times and knew it off by heart.

When Jaz had finished May 25th, Vic turned back to her.

"So", he said, "I've got to go back to get the piece of paper with the code on; the one that shows where the circles need to be positioned to open the great door. If I can get it, I'd at least end up with the last thing that dad drew, which would be special. But, more importantly, I think it's going to be essential if we are going to find them."

It was only then that it began to dawn on Jaz what may ultimately be in Vic's mind. And the fact that he had said the word "we" was somewhat disconcerting.

VR-K
The Combination

Vic wished he had a camera - one of those retro types that produce an actual photograph in a couple of minutes. It would have been great to have captured Jaz's priceless reaction as she watched Spike Sprite zoom down the purple tunnel.

As Spike blinked at Jaz through the screen, the colour drained out of her face making her dark eye shadow look even darker than normal. If her hair had not already been standing on end as a result of handfuls of gel, it would have risen of its own accord. To say she was shocked was an understatement.

Vic had already found the website for 'The World Institute for Objects of Antiquity' and for the third time had double clicked on the Guardian icon. The process did not feel at all strange to him anymore, but for Jaz it was proving a lot to take in.

Spike Sprite spoke first in a jingly jangle tone. "Greetings Vic, you are back a little sooner than the Guardian had expected! After your last two visits we wondered whether you would ever come back at all!"

"Try keeping me away" laughed Vic, "Anyway, I have some unfinished business at the Institute, and I need to return."

"No problem. I just hope for your sake that the ferocious guard dog is not around" said Spike with a wink.

Vic paused for a moment, not sure of what Spike's answer would be to his next question. He coughed a little to clear his throat and then spoke. "Spike is it possible to take anyone else with me when I travel in virtual reality?"

Spike did not seem at all surprised by the request. "Vic, it's your choice. Providing the person is holding your hand while the other one is being scanned, they will also be mutated into digital code."

At this point Jaz looked alarmed. Even though Vic had explained the process to her a few times he had never used the word 'mutate'. To her, it sounded like you could end up with two heads or a nose on your knee. However, for fear of appearing scared, which she actually was, she kept quiet.

Spike Sprite continued. "Everything is the same as before, so long as you use the VR tunnel sensibly, it will remain available to you. So, shall we all go?"

Vic was about to put his hand on the scanner when he suddenly remembered that Nana was in the other room. "Hang on a second" he said, and quickly went to check what she was doing.

She was dozing in the chair. The stressful events at Agnes Allsorts had clearly worn her out.

Even so, Vic knew he ought to ask her before leaving.

"Nana" he whispered.

She sighed in her sleep, licked her lips, and said something about 'dry roasted peanuts'.

"She must be dreaming" Vic deduced. Nevertheless, he asked the question, "Nana, do you mind if Jaz and I pop out for a bit?" It wasn't a lie, although it did stretch the truth a little!

Nana sighed again and mumbled, "Off you go, but don't forget to bring back some cashews". She was well gone, thought Vic!

He tiptoed back to the front room where Jaz was now deep in conversation with Spike. She was trying to grasp the technical bit about how the scanner changed you so that you could be transported in the bi-linear-digi-data-conduit.

"So, my cells and DNA get transformed into digital code; that's very wacky."

She turned and looked at Vic as he came back into the room. Vic laughed. "It's too tricky to understand, believe me. The best way is to try it out. You will understand it more when you've been in and out of the PC once."

Jaz was not completely convinced but nodded and agreed to give it a go.

With the image of the hallway at the Institute on screen, Vic placed his hand on the scanner and hit the 'Scan' button. Before Jaz could change her mind, he grabbed her hand with his other and whispered, "Hold tight".

Jaz stood motionless feeling the kind of fear that you experience just before you go on a 'white knuckle' roller coaster ride.

The strange sensations began for both of them at the same time.

First there were the unpleasant pins and needles in the toes that swiftly moved up their bodies. Vic could feel Jaz stamping her feet a little. Then they both began to be transformed into a shimmering mass of bright blue numbers. As the 0's and 1's reached their necks and the whooshing noise surrounded their heads, Jaz let out a high-pitched squeal.

Vic just had time to shout, "Hang on, here we go", and they were inside the computer. Without any further discussion Spike grabbed Jaz's other hand and they began hurtling down the purple tunnel. The acceleration was so incredible that it took all Vic's might to turn his head enough to see Jaz. At first, she screamed, but within seconds she was whooping with laughter!

The journey didn't take long and suddenly Vic saw the polished floor of the Institute heading towards them at the end of the tunnel. Having been caught out on all his previous VR trips, he started running in mid-air to try and keep his balance on landing.

As they shot out of the end of the tunnel, Vic, just managed to stay on his feet but watched Jaz rolling away at high speed across the floor towards the display cabinets.

"Nice landing Vic, you're getting the hang of this" encouraged Spike. "Now, I've had to move the portal for you to get back. The big plant has gone, so I've placed it under the display cabinet with the Roman mosaic. There's enough room for you both to squeeze under." And with that instruction, he was off.

Jaz came over rubbing her elbow, which had a nasty red friction burn after her spectacular skid.

Vic put his finger to his lips and said "Ssshhh". After the thrill of the VR journey, Jaz had completely forgotten that a large wolf called Fang was known to roam the premises. She nodded.

Vic whispered, "I think we should check the coast is clear before going into Uralt's office."

70

As it was 'after hours', it was likely that the only person around would be Knapper the Security Guard. But then again, after last time, Vic didn't want to take any chances. It would be a bit risky to check but Vic wanted to make sure who was in the building to avoid getting cornered in Uralt's office again.

On the wall was a sign and arrow that said, 'Security Office'. Vic and Jaz crept along a corridor in the direction in which it pointed.

The only illuminations were the green fire escape signs on the walls. The whole place felt really eerie. As they turned a corner, they could see a single light beaming from a hatch in the wall. Vic motioned with his hand that this was their destination. Having crawled up to the hatch they could see the sign 'Security Office' over the window. Holding their breath, they both rose slowly to peer through the glass like deep sea divers emerging from the deep.

Inside, all was peaceful. Knapper was asleep in a chair with his cap pulled down over his face. The small portable television in the corner of the room was still on.

As Vic rose higher, he could see Fang lying on the floor slobbering over a huge leg of meat. It was big enough to have come from a small dinosaur, or possibly a large burglar. Vic shuddered.

On the wall was a board with all the names of the staff who worked at the Institute. There were little signs next to each one that could be changed from 'In' to 'Out'. They all said 'Out' - the coast was clear!

Suddenly, Fang turned and looked at the hatch window. Vic dropped to the floor like a stone. He braced himself for a loud bark, but thankfully all remained silent. Vic did not dare check again and assumed Fang had returned to slobbering on the hunk of meat.

He indicated for Jaz to go back down the hallway and they both crept away.

The door to Professor Uralt's office was open and Vic switched on the desk lamp so that they could see what they were doing. He went straight over to the filing cabinet; there was no time to lose.

He pulled at the drawer marked 'Staff'. It opened about a centimetre and then stopped. It was locked! He tried it a couple of times in sheer disbelief, but each time it refused to budge. Vic looked at Jaz in horror.

Jaz tried to calm the situation. "There has got to be a key somewhere." Vic hoped she was right, but where could it be?

They both set to work in a desperate search for the key checking Uralt's desk, bookcases and under the many pot plants. After a couple of frantic minutes, they stopped and looked at each other. Vic shrugged his shoulders and was about to admit defeat.

Then, they both turned and focussed their eyes on a small carved African-looking pot sitting on top of the filing cabinet. It was an ugly little thing, so ugly that your eye tended to overlook it. They immediately thought the same thing and Vic grabbed it and removed the lid. There, to his relief, were a small bunch of keys nestling in the bottom of the pot.

With his hands shaking, Vic started trying the keys out. "Nope" he said under his breath as the first one refused to turn. "No. No. Nope." He turned to Jaz with a worried look on his face and held up the last key. He kissed it for good luck and pressed it into the filing cabinet lock. "Come on, come on" he whispered.

It turned!

Without a moment's hesitation Vic pulled open the squeaky drawer and ran his fingers over the name tabs on the files until his thumb fell on 'The Rostruns'. He scrabbled frantically through the contents until there, squashed between two letters, was the crumpled piece of paper with the five circles on.

"Yes!" he said triumphantly.

Even though they needed to get going, Vic could not resist a quick look.

There were five discs drawn in a circle. They looked a bit like the knobs on a cooker. Each of the five circles had a bird, the sun, a snake, a beetle and finally what looked like a mask with an angry face drawn on them. The circles each had a different symbol at the top.

Vic realised that Jaz was looking over his shoulder. She whispered, "It looks like the combination for a safe". Vic nodded; he'd thought exactly the same.

"Come on", he said, "We'd better get out of here before Fang goes for his walkies."

He carefully folded the sheet and put it in his pocket while Jaz shut the drawer, locked it, and returned the keys to the ugly little pot.

"Let's go" she said. Vic needed no encouragement. He switched off the lamp and they cautiously peered round the office door.

All was quiet.

Vic looked down towards the display cabinet with the Roman mosaic. There in the gloom, clear for them to see, was the shimmering blue dot on the floor.

Like 'cat burglars' they quickly and quietly made their way over to the cabinet and crawled underneath.

Vic sat down on the dot and grabbed Jaz's hand. He looked down at his trousers, which appeared to be pulsating with the blue light underneath.

Jaz giggled, "Look you've got a radioactive bum, what on earth did you have for lunch".

Vic smiled and was about to reply but Spike materialised, and they all disappeared.

VR-L

The Bullies

After the raid on the Institute, the thought of a day at school seemed very mundane. As Vic trudged along, his mind was on one thing and that wasn't learning. He couldn't get an image of his parents turning the stone circles and lining the Mayan symbols up out of his head.

He had already memorised the combination - bird, sun, snake, beetle, and mask. The mystery was what had then happened once the great stone door had opened. He had already considered a number of theories, none of which were very pleasant. But he hung onto the hope that somehow his parents were still alive somewhere.

As Vic neared the school, he had to pass down an alley between two rows of houses, which led down to the main gate. The fences were covered in multicoloured graffiti and there were always empty beer cans and cigarette butts on the ground from the local gangs that had been hanging around the night before.

As he turned into the alley his stomach went tight. There, hanging around menacingly at the other at the end of the alley, was Brian Bane. It was no coincidence, and it could only mean one thing: big trouble!

For Vic to turn around and walk the other way to school meant a huge detour. That would make him late and would result in a certain one-hour detention after school, which was a real nuisance. So, Vic decided that the preferred option was to encounter Bane, even though it would probably involve some form of horrendous hassle.

He tried to act 'cool' and walked boldly pretending either that he hadn't noticed Bane, or if he had, that he didn't care.

He was about two thirds of the way down the alley, too far from either end to make a run for it, when Bane moved into action. It was like a scene from a wildlife film where a lion lies motionless, except for its flicking tale, then suddenly leaps up to chase its prey.

Before Vic could escape, Bane had him backed up against the fence. He snarled menacingly in Vic's face. "So Vicky, been visiting virtual reality, have you?" he mocked. "I always knew you lived in another world you crank. Well, never mind virtual reality; try this for a bit of genuine reality!"

With that he spun Vic round and shoved him against the fence as hard as he could. Vic's face ended up squeezed against the wooden panel. It was rough and painful, and he could taste the creosote paint. Bane then bounced hard against him pushing the air out of his body. Like a balloon deflating Vic groaned and finally fell to the ground. He lay on his back completely winded.

Bane stepped back smiling, satisfied at the outcome. He looked down at Vic who was cowering in the mud and stood firmly on his thigh pinning him to the ground. "I'm gonna fix you and that computer of yours, twit-head" he warned. "So you'd better look out!" And with that, he strolled off kicking an empty lager can.

Vic got up and brushed himself down. His second-hand clothes were not the smartest at the best of times, but he could have done without rolling around on the wet ground. He looked dreadful! On one trouser leg there was now more mud than material showing, and he had a clear footprint from Bane's shoe on the other.

What made matters worse was that his first lesson was double history and Parson's was a stickler for tidiness. He expected everyone to look like their clothes had just been collected from the dry cleaners. 'Slacks', as he called trousers, should always have sharp ironed creases, just like the dreadful toffee-coloured ones that he always wore.

Vic feared that his filthy trousers would cause a 'pop-out' and he was right.

"Sit down and shut up this instant" roared Parsons as the class bundled into the room like a flock of sheep.

Vic, fearing a close inspection, tried to position himself behind the largest pupil in the class, a girl named Honour Atkins. However, despite the considerable and welcome cover that she provided, Parsons never missed a trick.

"Rostrun!" he screamed. "Come here boy, this instant."
Everyone scuttled to their seats grateful that it was Vic that had been
singled out for attention.

Things didn't look good. Parson's eyes were already bulging
before he had even uttered one word. There was to be no build up
from whispering to wrath, 'Pop-out' was already fit to explode.

He drew breath and then blasted. "Never in all my time at this
hallowed seat of learning have I ever seen a pupil in such a mess.
Rostrun, look at yourself, you are a disgusting little oik. You are a
disgrace to yourself, your class and the school!"

Vic could see beyond Parsons to Bane, who was almost falling
off his chair with silent laughter.

'Pop-out' was so angry that showers of spit were flying out with
the words, like an ornamental fountain.

"Rostrun, I refuse to teach you whilst you are wearing such
shoddy trousers. They clearly haven't seen an iron in weeks. They are
filthy and ... I don't believe it ... you even have a footprint on that leg.
Go into my cupboard where you will find a box of lost property.
Change into something else for the rest of this lesson, laddie."

Vic couldn't believe it. First, he had been bullied by Bane and
now by 'Pop-out', it just didn't seem fair.

He made his way into the dark and musty storeroom. Around
the walls were numerous shelves, groaning under the weight of old
history books that had bored generations of school pupils.

It was weird to see a secret side to Parson's world. He often
disappeared into the cupboard during lessons when the class was
copying huge chunks from textbooks. But no one knew exactly what
he did while he was in there.

There were all sorts of intriguing and terrible rumours, but the
truth was now clear to Vic. In the corner was a small table with a stack
of old 'Steam Railway Enthusiast' magazines, a kettle, mug, and very
old sandwich toaster.

Vic thought to himself "Flip, he comes in here for secret
snacks."

76

If you ever got caught eating in lessons, even sucking a mint, it was instant detention. However, 'Pop-out' obviously sloped off for mid-lesson feasts. He lifted the lid on the toaster. It was disgusting and had years of burnt-on cheese round the edges. It was enough to make you retch.

Vic thought he had better turn his attention towards looking for the lost property, box, before he got in any more trouble for dawdling. He found it behind the door, but, to his dismay, there was hardly anything that he could wear in place of his filthy trousers. The best thing he could find was a huge pair of white football shorts with a drawstring around the waist. They looked like something that would have been worn at a sports event in the 1900's. They came down well below his knees and even though he knew he looked really stupid, there was no option but to return to the class.

The roar that greeted him was deafening.

In response to the laughter, he pretended he was running out as a famous centre forward in a Victorian Cup Final. He could almost hear the cheers - "We love you Rostrun, we do, we love you Rostrun, we do." He jogged to his seat, but in the heat of the moment foolishly waved to the ecstatic crowd.

Parsons went red with rage and snapped the pencil he was holding clean in two.

"Rostrun! If you think this is some giant joke you are sorely mistaken. Back to the cupboard you insolent ignoramus and choose another garment – NOW!"

Vic turned and dashed back to the cupboard to the cheers of a few brave pupils, which were quickly silenced by a point of 'Pop-out's' bony finger.

To Vic's absolute horror the only other thing that could be worn on your lower half was a red PE skirt. There were plenty of odd socks and a few T shirts but no other shorts or tracksuit bottoms.

To disobey Parson's and return in the long shorts again was unthinkable. So, he had no option but to go back out with the girl's skirt on. He braced himself for 'Pop-out's' reaction.

This time the rage was volcanic. Parson's eyes came right out on stalks and Vic was sure he saw a puff of steam burst from under his collar. 'Pop-out' was about to go completely ballistic when in an instant he froze and then grinned an evil, vindictive smirk. "Yes. A skirt, that will do nicely. Now sit down and pay attention."

The lesson began.

"Civilisation. That is our next topic of study. I bet not many of you know what civilisation is, especially Rostrun. But in the next month we are going to learn about some of the great civilisations in history. Most are sadly no longer with us, and I wish the same were true of many of you!" He glared at Vic.

Then for the rest of the lesson, Parsons drew a 'timeline' on the board and listed when the famous civilisations in history existed.

Despite being a bit distracted by wearing a skirt, which was unusually draughty around the underwear zone, Vic actually found it interesting hearing about races like the Egyptians, Babylonians, Romans, Aztecs, and Incas. He knew this topic fascinated his parents and he found it really enjoyable too, so maybe he had inherited the interest.

For a few moments he daydreamed about where mum and dad might be. In his mind he saw the five circles that formed the combination to the great door in the Matapopafetal city in Guatemala. But that image didn't last long. Parsons raised his voice and Vic snapped back into reality.

"So, I know you are all desperate to hear what your next history project is." Everyone groaned, all except for Vic.

Parson's continued, "Each of you must prepare and give a five-to-six-minute presentation, and no waffle mind, on the topic 'The most amazing civilisation is ... ' and then you must explain your choice. Everyone will present their piece in front of the class on Friday. Any questions? No? Class dismissed!"

On the way out, Vic popped back into the cupboard to change back into his filthy trousers, but he didn't seem to notice Parsons' glare or even the mess on his leg; his mind was elsewhere.

After Vic had got home, changed his clothes and Nana had put his trousers in a bucket to soak, he went straight on the computer to begin his history project. He typed in an Internet enquiry on 'The Maya'. Within a second the search engine had delivered pages of fascinating information from around the world to his front room.

It took him about an hour to gather enough content for his talk, which he cut and pasted into the word processor. With a bit of editing and a couple of trial runs he soon had a presentation that ran almost exactly to time.

As there was still a bit of time before the mince, potatoes and peas were ready, he went back to look at the Mayan websites.

"How on earth can I find the lost city where mum and dad went?" he wondered. He searched the web again using the tribe's name Matapopafetal, but nothing came up. "It's probably because no-one knows anything about them", he thought, "Which is the very reason mum and dad went to Guatemala in the first place."

As a long shot, he searched under 'stone circles' but got a strange mixture of websites including one on Stonehenge. But none had anything to do with the crumpled piece of paper in his pocket.

He logged off the computer and went through for his tea.

As he chewed his mince, potatoes, and peas, he concluded that finding his mum and dad was not going to be as easy as he had hoped!

VR-M

The Presentation

Friday's history lesson came around all too quickly. Even though Vic had thoroughly prepared, the thought of standing up in front of the class, not to mention 'Pop-out', gave him butterflies in his stomach.

As Vic sat down there was a murmur of fearful anticipation. Everyone looked anxious. Even Bane looked edgy, and he usually feared nothing. This was not the first time the group had given presentations, and, on past form, they were about to get publicly humiliated. On the last occasion several pupils broke down in tears at the harshness of Parsons' comments. Not only did the content of your talk get marked, but 'Pop-out' was quick to criticise your tone of voice and even the way you stood. He missed nothing!

Vic could still remember the rebukes from last time. "Laddie, you look like a beggar in the street asking for loose change. Young lady your voice is like the feeble squeak of a mouse, too scared to come out of its hole. Boy, you are dressed like an untidy vagabond, why should I bother listening to you. Madam, I've found more interesting information on a cereal packet, sit down before I fall asleep".

The worst bit was that everyone had to laugh at the awful comments about their friends. It was vital to keep 'Pop-out' happy, even though it made their classmates feel dreadful.

Parsons had borrowed a small section of staging from the drama studio, together with some spooky scenery, and placed it at the back of the room. He had set his chair on it, raising him high above everyone else. He looked like an evil vulture sitting at the top of a tree viewing its prey. It made him seem even more intimidating than usual and gave him a clear view of the trembling presenters. There was no way to escape his piercing stare.

At the end of each talk he would wait a moment, leaving enough time for each pupil to quake in terror. Then he would clear his throat and shout out the mark and humiliating comment for all to hear, which was later added to the pupil's project in blood red ink.

It had been hard going up to Vic's turn. Most had got C's and D's and there was only one B for the class swot, Clive Grovlar-Jones. And that was only a B minus.

So, it was with some fear and trepidation that Vic stood up when his name was called and headed for the front of the class. By the time he turned to face Parsons he was so nervous and busting for the toilet. But the agonising tinkle would have to wait; there was no option but to cross his legs and begin.

"The most amazing civilisation is the Maya."

Parsons looked up slowly from his clipboard with a quizzical expression. He tugged at his eyebrow. So far, all but one person had chosen either the Egyptians or Romans.

Only Clive Grovlar-Jones had spoken on a different civilisation called the Assyrians, which Vic had never heard of. That earned him the B, but then he was a right boffin and always sucked up to the teachers, even 'Pop-out'.

For a brief moment Vic's sneaked a peak at Parsons. There was no doubt that he looked pleasantly surprised at his choice. It was a bit disconcerting, but it gave Vic encouragement to continue.

"The Mayan civilisation was one of the great ancient races. It dates as far back as 2600 B.C. It existed until around A.D. 900 when it strangely disappeared. (A bit like mum and dad thought Vic). Why that happened is a still a mystery.

The Maya lived in Central America. They settled across the countries that we now know of as Mexico, Guatemala, Belize, and Honduras. Much of this region is covered by impenetrable rain forests. That makes it quite challenging to exist there, even today.

Now, while much of today's hi-tech world was living in the Dark Ages with little technology, the Maya had achieved some amazing things. They had developed their own writing system and mathematic skills. They even had a calendar, which they lived by. They were so clever that even without the use of telescopes they managed to map the stars and the planets.

The Maya built the most incredible cities. They were not made of mud like other civilisations of their time, but of stone. They were designed using amazing geometric shapes such as pyramids, a bit like those of the Egyptians. Incredibly, they were constructed without the use of the equipment, which would be essential to undertake such a building project today.

They had no metal tools, wheels, or large animals to help them move the huge stones. How they managed this incredible feat is still a mystery, but that is the case with many things to do with the Maya (including mum and dad's disappearance, thought Vic).

In the earliest days, the Maya were farmers. They lived in the jungle and cleared areas of the forest to plant simple crops. The soil in most of the places they farmed was not very good. So, life for the average Mayan family was hard and they often had to move around.

Some of the Maya lived in regions where there were volcanoes. While the ash from the eruptions made the ground more fertile, it was obviously a dangerous place to live.

Around 2000 B.C. the Maya began to settle in villages. They planted crops such as maize, beans and tobacco. To make the most of the mountainous slopes they learned how to cut terraces into the hillsides. That gave them flat fields that were much easier to farm. These farming villages were the beginning of their great cities.

As the Maya civilisation developed, they learned new skills. They began to weave cloth and make pottery. This provided things that they could trade. So, they cleared paths through the jungle to do business with other tribes.

In the region there are also a number of rivers. These run from the mountains to the Pacific Ocean and the Gulf of Mexico, which lay either side of Central America. The Maya realised that water was a quicker means of transport than travelling through the jungle. So, they developed canoes to allow them to travel by river (just like mum and dad thought Vic).

Around 300 B.C. the Maya chose kings to rule their tribes. They also formed what is known as a 'hierarchy'. That made it clear which people in their community were the most important. First were the nobles or elders. They were followed by teachers, scribes, warriors, architects, craftsmen, labourers, and farmers.

Around 100 B.C. they started to build large cities. Most were near the rivers to help provide water. The cities became the centres for trade, farming and rituals and the population grew.

One of the largest cities, called Tikal, was built around 500 A.D. It had around 60,000 people; that's large even compared with most of our towns.

Most of the great Mayan cities rose majestically out of the jungle on stepped platforms. If you were to see a Mayan city for the first time, the great pyramid-shaped temples would immediately catch your eye. There were also grand palaces with courtyards, where the most important people lived.

If you ever got the chance to walk around a Mayan city, you would notice the beautiful carvings and paintings used to decorate the walls (just as mum and dad did, thought Vic to himself).

As there were often dry seasons, they built huge reservoirs to store enough water for the people to survive.

As the Maya now lived in different kingdoms, they began to develop many different languages.

They also had some amazing beliefs!

They thought the earth was flat and had four corners. Each of the corners was given a special colour. White for north, yellow for south, red for east and black for west. The middle of the flat earth was given the colour green.

Some Maya believed that the sky was held up at the corners by great trees. Others thought it was supported by four incredibly strong gods called 'Bacabs'. In fact, the Maya believed in all sorts of gods. They had over 160 different ones.

They also believed that some creatures had special powers. One in particular was the Quetzal, a rare bird. It had brilliant blue-green tail feathers, which were sometimes over half a metre in length. Maya kings wore these feathers as prized possessions. Sadly, today this bird is nearly extinct.

The Maya also developed an amazing writing system that had over 800 signs that could be combined to form their words. Archaeologists call these signs 'glyphs'. These glyphs were often carved in stone and wood, or painted on paper, walls, and pottery.

It is really hard to understand what glyphs mean. The letters of our alphabet have sounds, but each glyph symbol meant something. Even with the help of computers, archaeologists today are still struggling to work out Mayan writing.

The Maya loved mathematics, unlike me - to which there was laughter in the class and even Parsons smiled. Their counting system only had three symbols. A dot for a 1, a bar for 5 and a shell for 0.

Instead of a decimal counting system, which is based on the number 10, with 1's, 10's, 100's and 1,000's, they used a system based on the number 20, which went 1, 20, 400 and 8,000.

The number 20 was a sacred number as it was the number of fingers and toes that you could count on.

The Maya were great astronomers. They thought the stars and planets gave them wisdom and guidance. They built observatories to help them study the heavens and learned how to predict the movements of the constellations and solar and lunar eclipses.

From these studies they developed accurate calendars. In fact, the earliest known solar calendars were found carved in stone dating back to around 400 B.C.

Some Mayan murals and carvings show people wearing symbols of the Sun, Moon and Venus, which was a particularly important planet to them.

For some reason, around A.D. 900, the Maya abandoned their cities, and the civilisation began to decline. No one is quite sure why. To this day it remains an unsolved mystery.

By around A.D. 1200, the Mayan dynasty had all but disappeared. Today, the ancestors of the Maya now mainly live in Peru and Mexico. But the great cities lay deserted in the remote and dense jungles of Central America."

When Vic had finished, he took a deep breath and awaited the verdict. There was an agonising pause. Vic could feel his heart pounding.

'Pop-out' finished scribbling on his mark sheet. He slowly raised his head.

"Well Rostrun", he said, "That was surprisingly good. I award you a B plus."

The whole class gasped in disbelief.

Vic couldn't believe his ears. A B plus was the best you could get with Parsons. He returned to his seat in a complete daze whilst Clive Grovlar-Jones gnashed his teeth at being beaten.

The next person up was Honour Atkins. The pressure of the presentation was causing streams of sweat to pour down her face. She looked like she had just washed her hair! She rustled her papers nervously and began in a croaky voice.

"The most amazing civilisation is the Babylonian empire. Its cities could be found by the river Euphrates."

At the mention of the phrase 'found by the river', Vic sat bolt upright in his seat. It was all he could do to prevent himself from leaping up and shouting "Yes!"

That was the last thing that he heard of her presentation. Those four words had triggered a thought in his mind. They had solved the problem that had been frustrating him for days.

"That's it", he said, under his breath, "All I need to do is to go on the Internet. The city can be found by the river!"

VR-N
The Lost City

Nana had been asleep for at least an hour when Vic crept downstairs dressed in a white tee shirt, khaki shorts, socks, and boots. All he needed was an old-fashioned pith helmet and he would have looked like a true explorer.

Vic knew that the VR trip he was about to embark on was far more dangerous than the visits to the Institute, so he had decided to go it alone, even though he would have valued Jaz's company.

He switched on the computer and once the Internet search engine had loaded, he typed in 'River Fuddi'. He felt sure that he could find the city if he could only find the river.

The computer seemed to think for what seemed like ages but then, to Vic's delight, it returned a couple of hits. The better of the two was a conservation website which showed a couple of pictures of the Fuddi in a discussion about endangered rainforests.

One picture showed the river as a wide estuary and the colour of chocolate milkshake. Vic thought that if he went there, it may take weeks to walk to the city. He needed a picture near the source of the river, where his parents had abandoned their canoe.

Thankfully, the other photograph showed the Fuddi as a smaller river with vines hanging down from the forest canopy. It looked dark and dangerous - the kind of place that you would find snakes that could swallow you whole. Vic shuddered, but he knew that was where he needed to head.

So, he loaded that image of the River Fuddi on the screen.

Before heading off, he popped into the kitchen and took two bags of crisps, one cheese and onion and the other prawn cocktail, which he stuffed into a small rucksack together with a bottle of water. He knew he couldn't travel to the jungle without adequate supplies.

So, equipped for the excursion, he clicked on the Guardian icon and placed his hand on the scanner.

The sight of Spike Sprite zooming down the purple tunnel sent a tingle down his spine. Spike peered through the monitor. "A visit to the jungle" he jangled, "Another school project or are you on a different sort of mission?"

It was weird. Vic hardly knew Spike, but he trusted the Sprite. So, he decided to tell Spike all about his parents.

After the explanation, which took a couple of minutes, Spike winked. "Perhaps the lightning strike on your house was no accident. Maybe the Guardian meant you to gain access to VR to sort things out".

Vic got the distinct impression from the twinkle in Spike's eyes that there was more going on that he realised.

"Is the Guardian that powerful?" enquired Vic.

"It's hard to explain" Spike replied, "But there are multi-dimensional links throughout the universe and virtual world that are beyond your comprehension. The Guardian's ways are far higher than yours and they would even frazzle the logic of Portal Sentries and we've seen the Guardian at work!"

"What is he like?" enquired Vic.

"Well, the Guardian is not a 'he' like you would think of a person. It exists in this extraordinary domain that looks like ..." Spike stopped and scratched his cube-like head. "Imagine you were inside a huge bubble watching all those rainbow colours moving around on the surface, well, the Guardian's domain is a bit like that. It observes images of every Internet interaction that takes place and every connection between the virtual and real world - your world. They are displayed all around the domain. The Guardian doesn't control everything, but it links things in such an unbelievable way that the best outputs are achieved. It's a sort of artificial intelligence."

"Flip" marvelled Vic, "You've completely lost me!"

"Never mind" laughed Spike, "It probably will never make sense. All you need to know is that the Guardian wants the best for you! So, are you ready for the jungle?"

With his hand on the scanner and his rucksack on his back, Vic hit the 'Scan' button. Pins and needles! Whirling numbers! The tunnel! Incredible speed! Then, before he could draw breath, Vic was sprinting through dense undergrowth with Spike by his side.

He stopped and listened. The air was hot and alive with the sound of chirping insects. Then, as if to warn of their arrival, a colourful bird high above squawked.

"This is amazing" Vic whispered, looking up and turning a full circle. Sunlight broke through the canopy of trees high above them and glinted on Spike's metallic body.

"OK" said Spike, "I've placed the portal in that old boat over there." Vic spun round and looked in the direction that Spike was pointing. There, by the side of the stream, covered in vines, was a battered old canoe.

Vic sprinted over and stared at it. For about thirty seconds he didn't move a muscle or even blink!

He turned to Spike. "This is spooky. It's my parents' boat, isn't it?"

Spike nodded.

Vic continued "Is the Guardian helping me more than I know?"

Spike thought for a moment and replied, "Ever since your computer was struck by lightning the Guardian has taken an interest in your plight. Whilst it cannot live your life for you, it will help you to reach your destiny by giving you the right opportunities."

Vic probed: "How? By making sure the right pages come up in my Internet searches?"

"Exactly" replied Spike "And, also I'm instructed to position the portal entrances strategically so as to help you stay on track, like here by the canoe."

"So" enquired Vic, "Am I going to find my parents?"

With that, Spike disappeared.

Vic took a sip of water from his bottle and pondered the hidden help. Then, he set out and began looking for the trail, his father had written about in his diary.

It wasn't that obvious, but he soon found a narrow path where the undergrowth had clearly been trodden down. It was odd. Here he was in the middle of nowhere and yet someone must have passed that way quite recently. It was the only explanation for the flattened plants.

Vic stood absolutely still, half expecting to see some eyes peering at him through a bush. But, apart from the chirping insects, he was quite alone.

He started out on the trail. It was horrendously humid and within seconds sweat was pouring from his body, soaking his shirt.

He stopped for another swig of water and then followed the trail for another ten minutes until he met a wall of densely growing trees.

They seemed to prevent his progress and there seemed nothing to do but turn back. But then he stopped. "This has to be the way" he thought, so with lots of grunting he pushed his way through the branches.

There, to his amazement, in a huge clearing, was the deserted city. He could hardly believe his eyes. One minute there was jungle, the next, huge stone ruins.

It was not a massive city like Tikal, which he had seen pictures of while doing his research, but it was big enough to cover an area of about four football pitches.

Vic ran forward and crouched by one of the pillars that once would have held up the massive gates to the city entrance.

There was absolutely no sign of life except for a few birds circling lazily in the sky above the clearing. Even though the place seemed deserted, Vic wanted to make sure before going any further. Something had happened to his parents here, so he needed to be wary.

Not knowing what might happen next, he thought it wise to have something to eat, so he took the prawn cocktail crisps out of his pocket. He sucked each crisp to prevent a crunch that could give his presence away to anyone hidden nearby.

From behind the pillar he viewed the breath-taking scene. The city was built on two levels and towering above all the other buildings was a pyramid shaped temple.

Like a cat seeking a mouse, Vic's eyes moved back and forth across the city looking for the slightest movement. But all was quiet and still.

After finishing the crisps, he licked his fingers and decided it was safe to move into the city for a closer look.

He crept around the ruined buildings. Despite the desolation, it was clear to see the houses and sizeable courtyards with tiled floors.

"In its day, this place must have been heaving with people" thought Vic.

As he investigated, he imagined traders selling their wares, astronomers studying charts of the night sky and rulers walking grandly by in rich robes.

Like spokes on a wheel, all the streets led to the temple at the centre of the city, so, it seemed the obvious place for Vic to head. After a few minutes he climbed the steps that led up to the large square from which the temple rose.

The sun was scorching hot, and Vic stopped for another glug of water, which was now unpleasantly warm.

There was not much on the temple plateau, just a big empty space. "More than enough room for several thousand people to gaze at the stars or observe an eclipse" thought Vic.

However, around the edge of the huge courtyard there were a number of raised areas, each with their own set of steps. Vic counted them - one, two, three, four, five!

He instinctively knew what they were and sprinted to the nearest one and bounded up the steps. Sure enough it was one of the sundials that his dad had written about. It was like a large round table with a stone gnomon in the centre casting a clear shadow in the blazing sunlight.

Vic ran his hand over the dial, touching the intricately carved stone beetle. It was amazingly lifelike, and it would not have surprised Vic if it had scurried away at his touch.

He ran to each of the other areas and sure enough he found the symbols of the bird, sun, snake, and mask that were etched on the crumpled scrap of paper in his pocket.

It felt very strange to be standing exactly where his parents had once stood.

Vic looked up purposefully, knowing his next move. He jogged to the temple pyramid and worked his way around the four stepped sides until he found the large, sealed door.

Beside it, exactly as he had imagined, were five stone discs like the knobs on a cooker. Each stone dial had five images carved on their surface and above them on the wall of the temple was a crescent moon marking where to line up the correct symbol.

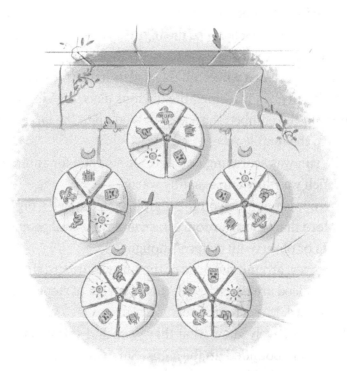

Maths wasn't Vic's favourite subject, but he realised there must be no end of combinations, so how on earth had his mum cracked the code? He could only think that it must have been something to do with the order of the sundials around the courtyard.

He carefully took the crumpled piece of paper out of his pocket. The pencil drawings had faded because he had looked at the diagram so often, but it didn't matter - he knew the dial positions off by heart.

Like a thief breaking into a safe, Vic carefully turned the dials to the correct positions. First, he lined up the bird with the moon. The disc rotated with a grinding noise as stone moved against stone. The second disc required the sun to be lined up with the moon. Then he positioned the snake, beetle and finally the angry-faced mask.

Vic held his breath.

For a moment nothing happened, but then there was a groaning noise deep within the pyramid. Vic gasped as the huge stone door began to open slowly, from bottom to top. He watched its progress, until it eventually halted above him with a deep-sounding clunk.

He stood, aghast. There before him was a sandy tunnel sloping down with fiery torches on the walls to provide some light. He could count four torches as he peered into the darkness, but he could see no further.

"Hello!" he called out into the cavernous black opening, hoping for friendly reply. He heard his voice echoing deep into the temple "Hello ... hello, ... hello".

He waited, but there was no answer.

VR-O

The Labyrinth

It took a few seconds for Vic's eyes to adjust to the darkness and his nose to the smell. The tunnel had the pong of a hamster cage that hadn't been cleaned for a month.

Vic could feel his heart pounding. He had no idea of what he was about to encounter. It must have been the same for his parents, but what was worrying was that they had never returned.

He slowly crept forward.

After about fifty metres, the tunnel separated into four entrances. Each had a menacing mask and Mayan glyphs above the openings. He had a quick peep through one doorway which immediately branched into three other tunnels. It looked like he was about to enter a labyrinth obviously intended to complicate things for unwelcome guests.

Vic guessed that the glyphs must give clues to the safe route through - but they were of little use to him. For all he knew he was about to walk into a trap, destined to become lunch for some wild animal that roamed the labyrinth! The other alternative was that he walked around aimlessly until he starved. He shuddered at the thought of both outcomes.

But he had come this far and there was no choice but to pick an entrance and hope for the best.

He was about to make a random selection when he got a flash of inspiration. He remembered doing a school project on mazes and his teacher at the time, Mr Elfinwinkle, had explained ways to make sure that you got out safely.

"Now what were they?" thought Vic.

To jog his memory, he pictured Elfinwinkle holding up a ... now what was it? A ball of string - that was it!

Elfinwinkle had explained that you unwound string as you went, so you could retrace your steps to safety. But that was no good, the nearest thing he had was a shoelace and that wouldn't get him far.

However, there was another method. Vic racked his brain.

"Got it!" he cried triumphantly. Elfinwinkle had also walked round the classroom with his hand on the wall. He said that providing you didn't take your hand off as you walked, you would eventually cover all the options and find the exit.

Vic chose the doorway on the right; it seemed as good as any. He placed his hand on the wall and entered the labyrinth. Within seconds, the soft chalky wall had turned his palm as white as a gymnast's about to grasp the parallel bars.

The labyrinth quickly became very dark, so, at the first opportunity, Vic grabbed one of the torches hanging on the wall. He hadn't thought about it before, but it was weird how they kept burning. They gave off a smell like the science labs at school and were obviously soaked in some strange chemical that enabled them to burn for ages. But, then again, they couldn't possibly burn forever. It made Vic convinced that the city was inhabited.

He glanced over his shoulder, half expecting to see someone following him, but he was alone. He waved the torch around in the darkness - it felt comforting to have it.

Vic continued. He did not end up going down too many 'dead ends', then suddenly the passage began to narrow. It was not enough to prevent his progress, but plump Uncle Collingwood would have certainly got stuck and fired off a loud biffy in his attempt to get free.

Soon the tunnel became so tight that Vic had to hold the torch above his head to prevent his elbow from scraping on the wall. As he edged forward, he looked up to make sure that the burning embers didn't fall onto his head. He watched them dancing in the darkness above him.

Then, without warning, Vic stumbled. The floor had gone!

For a moment he wobbled like an acrobat missing their step on the high wire. He just managed to get his weight onto his left foot, which was still on firm ground, and kicked out karate-style with his right foot, which was now swinging in mid-air. The move was just enough to propel him backwards onto the passage floor.

For a few seconds he lay there with his heart pounding. He picked up the torch, which he had flung away during the mid-air dance, and crept forward to where he had almost fallen.

Now that he was looking down, it was clear to see that the passage floor disappeared for a few metres ahead. It was too dark to see how deep the pit was, so Vic carefully lay down at the edge of the abyss and pointed the flaming torch into the darkness. It lit the gloom with a ray of light, like a lighthouse beam cutting through a pitch-black stormy night. The pit was about three metres deep, with sheer sandy sides. If he had fallen in, there would have been no way out.

Then, out of the corner of his eye, just beyond the beam of light, he sensed movement. He swished the torch round and there to his horror, in the corner of the pit, were three huge black snakes coiled together in a writhing pile. Their piercing eyes focussed menacingly on him. Suddenly, as if one creature, they hissed together and revealed their fearsome fangs at the sight of a possible meal.

Vic recoiled from the edge of the pit. He knew some snakes could spit lethal venom and he was not going to hang around to see if these ones could!

He stood up and considered his options. There seemed little point going back and checking what the other passages held in store. They could have worse horrors like spiders the size of dinner plates, running all over the floor, walls, and ceilings. That sent a cold tingle down his spine; he struggled with even a tiny spider in the sink at home.

So, he made the decision to somehow get over the pit and its hideous, hungry inhabitants.

It wasn't going to be easy because the narrow passage made a good jump almost impossible. The slightest bump on the wall would plunge him to a certain and gruesome death.

Vic quickly came up with a plan and walked up to the edge of the pit. With his back pressed against one wall, he quickly brought his legs up and forced his feet against the other. He was just big enough to bridge the gap and sat there, wedged above the abyss.

Gradually he slid his back along the wall, then his feet, then his back, then his feet again. His progress was slow and made even more difficult by the torch he was clinging on to. With each shift of his body the surface of the sandy wall crumbled into the darkness.

By halfway, every muscle in his body felt like it was on fire, however, to drop now would result in a grisly death. Vic, wedged between the walls, stopped, and shone the torch into the pit. Six green eyes glinted back, tracking his progress.

Bit by bit, Vic edged towards safety until the ravenous reptiles realised that their meal had passed and slithered into a gap in the pit wall. Vic dropped into a heap on the dusty floor on the other side of the chasm. His legs quivered uncontrollably from the unusual exercise, which had been tougher than any sports session at school.

He propped himself up on one elbow and took the bag of cheese and onion crisps out of his rucksack. The sight of the familiar blue bag was comforting in such bizarre circumstances.

He devoured the now smashed-up crisps and then scrunched up the empty bag and threw it in the pit. "Enjoy the meal losers" he laughed.

Vic drained the last drops of warm water from his bottle and then continued carefully along the corridor. To his amazement it narrowed even more, and he had to turn sideways to proceed. Then, in the gloom, Vic could see that the tunnel was coming to a sudden end. Sure enough, he found himself standing in front of what seemed like a solid wall.

After what he had just been through it was enough to make him weep or scream, or both. It seemed like the labyrinth had defeated him and there was no option but to turn back and try a different route.

He put his dusty hand on the end wall and was about to turn back to face the pit again when his fingers fumbled upon some holes. He held the torch closer and sure enough there were more than just one, in fact there were quite a number, just big enough to get your fingers in.

He put his index finger in one and wiggled it. The holes had a bottom; in fact as he pushed his finger in, the bottom gave way. He tried another and the same thing happened.

"Secret buttons" he whispered to himself, "But what for?"

He eased himself back and, using the torch, worked his way across the narrow wall.

On closer inspection there were twenty holes in all and each one had a tiny engraving next to it made up of lines and dots.

They seemed familiar and for a moment Vic couldn't think why. Then it came to him – hey were Mayan numbers. His mind flashed back to his presentation. He slowly recited the relevant section, which he knew off by heart.

"The Maya also loved mathematics. Their counting system only had three symbols: a dot for a 1, a bar for 5 and a shell for 0."

He crouched on the floor and tried to think logically. The numbered buttons must do something. His hunch was that they would open a secret door, but how? At first, he pressed his fingers randomly into lots of holes, but nothing happened. So, he thought carefully again about his presentation.

"The number 20 was a sacred number as it was the number of fingers and toes that you could count on."

"Twenty, perhaps that's the key" he said hopefully. He sprang up and looked at the holes and buttons again.

Using the Mayan symbols, he worked out that all the buttons were a 1, 2, 3, 4 or 5. There was no button for 20, so the only option was to make it by adding those on offer.

There were different ways to do this, but the problem was that the buttons were spread all over the wall making it difficult to push the necessary ones at the same time. Vic attempted a few options, but it was impossible to stretch your fingers wide enough.

Then, as if someone had switched a light on, he suddenly saw the solution. There were only four holes with the symbol of a bar, indicating a number 5, next to them.

As if he were reciting maths tables, he said out loud "Four fives are twenty."

The four buttons were grouped in two pairs, close enough to stick two fingers in from each hand.

Vic positioned his fingers like crabs' claws and with all his might thrust them into the holes. In the hope that it may help, he called out "Twenty", as if it were a secret password.

Within seconds there was a rumbling sound similar to when the temple door had opened. Then, the whole wall began to slide to one side. Vic could see no mechanism, but it moved as smoothly as the hi-tech glass doors on modern offices.

Vic stepped inside.

It was amazing. Around the walls of the large secret room before him were fearsome statues of Mayan warriors, wearing masks, with bodies covered in war paint, all standing on stone plinths. Vic marvelled; they seemed so lifelike.

The floor was equally breath-taking. It was a marvellous mosaic made of thousands of blue, mustard, and crimson tiles.

He bent down and wiped his hand across the polished tiles, which were as clean as the floor in Nana's kitchen, and she mopped that daily.

It was curious, how could it be so shiny! He was in an ancient, ruined city.

Unbeknown to Vic, two of the Mayan statues slowly turned their masked heads to observe him.

"Surely" Vic mused to himself, "This place can't be deserted, it's far too clean. Someone must have been here?"

He looked round and gasped!

Two razor sharp spears were pointing at his head and two of the plinths were now empty. Someone certainly did live here, and their eyes burned angrily from behind their hideous warrior masks.

He was a prisoner!

VR-P

The Courtroom

For the best part of an hour Vic waited in a tiny prison cell.

It was really eerie! As it was underground, there was no natural light and the flickering torches cast scary shadows on the dusty floor.

The only window was in the heavy door. It was about the size of a chessboard, although as Vic stared at the two vertical and horizontal bars, it looked more like a noughts and crosses game. While he waited, he played a few pointless matches against himself, which he won each time!

Vic looked down at the orange and brown woven Mayan tunic he had been ordered to put on by the guards. It was like an old-fashioned nightshirt that came down below his knees.

Here he was in the middle of the jungle, inside a secret city and he still had to wear terrible clothes! The shirt was the sort of weird garment that you would find at Agnes Allsorts. Many a time he had seen people shriek with delight having found such a daft piece of clothing to wear for a fancy-dress party.

However, judging by the number of gruesome skulls hanging around the walls of the cell, his unfashionable shirt was the least of his worries!

Suddenly, there was movement outside the cell, and he heard the heavy wooden bar being lifted from behind the door. It then opened with an agonising creaking noise as it swung open on its ancient wooden hinges.

There stood the two guards with their menacing masks and sharp spears. They gestured with the weapons for Vic to go with them. Trying to look really confident, he kicked his normal clothes into the corner and took his place between them.

Even though the guards looked fierce, they were not that much taller than Vic. For a moment, he thought about making a dash to escape, but then he saw the sticky tips on the spears. He guessed they were coated with a deadly poison, probably the venom from a jungle snake or the skin of a brightly coloured frog, so he decided to obediently march in time with their dusty feet into the unknown.

The destination was a large room, but this room was far grander than the first that Vic had seen. The walls were covered with murals of great battles and the ceiling had pictures of the sun, moon, and stars. At the far end there was a large wooden seat carved from a vast tree trunk and above the seat was draped a deep red canopy.

"The king's throne?" thought Vic. His stomach fluttered at the thought of meeting a real Mayan king, not to mention his fate having done so. He knew they could be fearsome tyrants.

He quickly tried to make up a speech to explain his presence in the temple, but he didn't get any time to think. As roughly as in the session with Brian Bane in the alley, the guards pushed Vic down and pressed his face against the cool tiles.

Someone then blew an ancient sounding trumpet, which sounded like an animal horn, Vic thought, and he could hear a group of people entering the room.

A voice boomed out in a language that Vic did not understand. Then, a softer voice translated the command: "Stand before King Quaxitopal of the Matapopafetal."

Vic was taken aback by their knowledge of his nationality; how did they know he was English? He stood up as straight as a soldier on guard duty and saw the King seated on the throne with several masked servants around him. One fanned him with a huge leaf from a jungle tree and another held a tray of delicious fruit.

Vic's stomach rumbled so loudly that the servants' heads jerked around. They glared at him from behind their masks and shook their heads in disbelief.

Realising his rudeness, Vic cleared his throat and spoke, "Forgive me your Majesty; I haven't eaten much today apart from two bags of crisps."

The English speaker translated, and the King reached out a hand and picked a peeled mango from the tray and tossed it towards Vic.

Like a cricketer fielding in the 'slips', Vic instinctively dived low and thrust out his right hand. He caught the fruit just before it hit the floor. It was an impressive catch that would have earned a slow-motion replay on television.

The King roared with laughter and clapped his hands above his head.

Vic assumed the applause was for his amazing acrobatics but when all the servants began to scurry away, he realised it was a signal to clear the room.

He munched the sticky, sweet mango as the servants left.

The only one that remained was the servant who translated the King's words.

For a moment, Vic's eyes focussed on the servant. It was odd. On closer inspection he was taller than the others, even the King, and his skin was much paler. But, before Vic could analyse the stranger anymore, the King spoke, and the tall, pale servant translated.

"Who are you, and why are you here?"

Vic took a deep breath and in his most polite English said, "I am Victor Rostrun and I come in peace." He couldn't remember where he had heard the phrase before, but it sounded good.

The tall pale servant reported the phrase to the King who then indicated that Vic should continue.

"Your Majesty, many years ago my parents came to explore this region. They were ... (then Vic thought for a moment, he didn't know for certain that they had died so he changed his words) ... they are famous explorers and wanted to find the lost tribe of the Matapopafetal. However, they never came back. I don't know whether they are still alive, so I set out to find them."

The tall pale servant translated but curiously kept his masked eyes on Vic the whole time.

The King thought for a moment and spoke. Vic waited for the English version.

"So, what would you do if you found them?"

Without a moment's hesitation Vic replied, "Your majesty I would take them home."

"But what if they were prisoners and not free to return with you?" came an angrier reply.

As the tall pale servant was uttering the final word the King leapt from his throne and triumphantly tore the mask from the servant's face.

He laughed a mocking laugh that reminded Vic of 'Pop-out' Parsons.

Vic stared at the pale servant with eyes like saucers and his mouth as wide as a railway tunnel. The pale servant spoke. Vic had often dreamt that one day he would hear these words.

"Vic, it's me, dad. I am alive."

There was a stunned silence which neither the King, Vic nor his father knew how to break.

Vic cried out "Is mum here too, is she still alive?"

"Yes" his dad replied, "She's fine and also works as a slave for the King."

In sheer delight, Vic did a crazy dance on the spot as if his pants were on fire.

The King cleared his throat loudly and Vic's dad remembered his duty. He spoke to the King in the foreign but now familiar sounding language. The King nodded a huge single nod.

Vic's dad turned to him, "I've asked if we may have some time alone together so that I can explain the situation."

The King moved to leave the courtroom and Vic felt a sharp shove from his father. He immediately followed his example and bowed low.

As soon as the King had left, Vic's dad motioned for them to sit down quickly on the mosaic floor.

"Vic, I can't believe you are here. I never thought I would see you again." He gave him such a huge hug that Vic let out a big burp. "It must be the mango" joked dad, and they both laughed.

"Now I'd better explain fast. Quaxitopal is ruthless and I don't know how much time we've got. Then, if there's time, you tell me how you found us." Vic nodded.

Dad continued. "Mum and I obviously found the tribe of the Matapopafetal but there were only a few people left: fifty at most. They live in this underground city, which extends beneath all you can see above ground. They built a warren of rooms and tunnels many centuries ago. It can only be reached through a complex labyrinth with many hidden dangers. Over the years many a tomb raider has come to a gruesome end."

Vic nodded and pictured the three snakes that had nearly had him for lunch.

"They even have a huge underground reservoir to provide fresh water. The only time they venture above ground is under the cover of darkness to tend the crops that they plant in clearings in the jungle, and for important ceremonies."

Vic couldn't help but interrupt, "But why do they live underground when there is such a beautiful city right above our heads?"

"Well" continued Vic's dad, "That was exactly what we wondered and having been here for a few years and learned the local language we have found out. It seems that the mystery as to why the great Mayan civilisation disappeared from the face of the earth is probably down to three reasons."

In the doorway to the courtroom there were some shadowy movements. Their conversation may be about to end, so Vic's dad hurried on. "According to Mayan history there were fierce wars between the tribes over land and wealth. These wiped out most of the young men so that there were few to become fathers.

At the same time the climate got much hotter. There were terrible droughts and the crops failed year after year. There were just too many mouths to feed, and many people starved.

Then explorers came, the Conquistadors from Spain, who ruthlessly plundered their belongings. Their only hope of survival was to hide. That's when this amazing underground city was built, and the tribe has lived in hiding ever since.

"Now the tribe has a legend that one day a pale skinned warrior would come, to solve their troubles. This warrior, called Tapta Papta, would bring with him great riches, power and everlasting food that would never run out. When we finally made it through the labyrinth, the King thought I was Tapta Papta. But when I had no riches, power, or amazing food, he was furious and made us slaves."

"So Vic" enquired his dad, "How on earth did you get here and work out all the Mayan codes?"

Vic didn't know where to start. He took a deep breath. "Well, it's all down to virtual reality. You see Collingwood bought me this brilliant computer to help with my schoolwork. Then, the house got struck by lightning; but don't worry Nana's fine because she hid under the stairs. Anyway, the lightning activated a portal on the PC into virtual reality, which I can now use. And the Guardian has been guiding me to help find you."

"Whoa!" exclaimed his dad. He reached out and felt Vic's brow. "Have you got jungle fever?"

"No, honest dad, its true!"

At that moment there was a loud clap, and the King strode back into the room followed by a line of servants.

The Rostruns bowed.

The King barked an order and Vic's dad returned to his side. There was more talking and then the translation came.

"Young man, even though I could make you a slave, because of your bravery in completing the labyrinth, I shall let you go, but your parents will stay."

Vic fell on his knees and pleaded, "Your Majesty, surely there must be something I can do to gain their freedom?"

The King listened to Vic's dad and then rubbed his chin in deep thought. Slowly, he rose from his throne, looked directly at Vic, and spoke in a hushed tone.

Vic's dad shook his head in dismay.

"What is it" cried Vic, "What must I do?"

His father turned to him; "The only thing which can gain our release is for you to complete The Quest and that means finding Tapta Papta. And that's the impossible challenge which Quaxitopal is going to offer you!"

VR-Q

The Quest

Vic watched intently as the servants formed a row from the doorway to his side. Then, through the doorway, a small stool appeared. The first servant in the row looked at the ceiling with an agonized expression, gave out a loud cry and then passed it to the next person. It was quickly grabbed and then with an equally loud cry it moved on again. It looked a bit like a weird game of pass the parcel.

As the stool got nearer, Vic could see that it was about the size of Nana's pouffe, as she called it, which she rested her frequently swollen feet on. However, the Mayan stool was much grander than the fake brown leather pouffe at home and was richly embroidered with images of plants and animals. After the final cry, Vic was offered the stool from the last servant in the line. He felt the servant's hands shaking violently as he passed it over.

Vic found it hard to understand why passing a stool would cause so much anxiety. That was, until his dad explained.

"You have just witnessed the solemn ritual that takes place when this stool, 'The Seat of the Sacred Quest', is brought into the courtroom. The Seat is looked upon with dread by the tribe because of the fearsome Quest that is associated with it. Anyone wishing to undertake The Quest, which is being offered to you, can only receive the instructions when seated on this stool."

Vic wasted no time and sat down before the King.

Quaxitopal clapped his hands slowly three times. Immediately, three female servants dressed in gold tunics, veils and headdresses walked into the room with great ceremony. Without a command, everyone bowed to the ground. From his seated position, Vic did his best to bow as well.

When everyone rose, Vic could see that the servant in the middle was carrying a solid gold tray encrusted with jewels that sparkled like stars on a frosty night. On the tray was an ancient scroll, which was passed to the King.

It was then that Vic suddenly noticed who the servant with the tray was, as she had paler skin than the other two. He was just about to leap up and shout "Mum" when he remembered how serious an event this was. So, he decided to keep quiet.

Vic's mum's eyes were visible behind the veil. She had always been an expert at communicating her feelings without having to say anything. If Vic was ever naughty while they were out, one look was enough to say, "Stop that now, or face the consequences when you get home!"

As Vic looked across the courtroom, her expression said everything that he needed to know. Vic winked back; it must have looked a bit silly, but it was all he could think to do.

As he watched, her eyes went cloudy and then several large tears fell like raindrops from behind the veil. Vic sensed they were tears of relief that he was all right.

King Quaxitopal stood up and unrolled the scroll.

Vic heard all the servants gasp and mutter.

In a loud voice, like a Toastmaster at a banquet he read out "The Quest". It didn't take that long, which encouraged Vic, as perhaps that meant that there was not too much to do.

Then his dad translated.

"The Quest is a challenge to reveal the one who is called Tapta Papta. It requires signs to be brought that show wealth, power, well-being, and insight.

The signs chosen by the ancient kings and elders are: For wealth - a carved goblet of finest jade. For power - the brightly coloured tail feather of the Quetzal bird. For well-being – a food which though eaten, will never run out. And, for insight - all three things must be presented on the golden tray at the moment the sun turns black.

To accept 'The Quest' and then return without all the elements or at the wrong time will result in death. To complete 'The Quest' means that the long awaited Tapta Papta has come. Then the King will give up the Sacred Throne for ever."

Vic took a deep breath. He understood bits of The Quest. He remembered that he had seen a Quetzal bird on the Internet whilst he was doing his history project, although it had said they were almost extinct. But a food that could be eaten but which never runs out just sounded like a riddle.

Without allowing any more time to think, King Quaxitopal asked for a response.

Vic's dad enquired, "Do you accept 'The Quest'?"

Every eye in the courtroom was fixed on Vic. Not one blinked. Vic could hear his heart thumping and his top lip was sweaty and tasted of salt.

"Your Majesty" replied Vic, "Until today I had never heard of Tapta Papta. I'm pale skinned, brave, and successfully made my way through your labyrinth. Whether I am Tapta Papta or not, only time will tell but for the fortune of my parents I accept 'The Quest'."

Following the translation there were gasps of surprise and Vic could see the astonishment on the faces of his parents. The King rose, raised both his hands, and shouted out a command.

"Let 'The Quest' begin!" declared Vic's dad.

Everyone shrieked and formed a circle around Vic. They sang and hopped madly as if the floor had suddenly got too hot to stand on.

Then, after a minute of madness, the servants formed a line and danced a sort of conga out of the room leaving just Vic, his parents, the King and the two guards with the sticky-tipped spears.

The King spoke, and dad translated: "I wish you well on 'The Quest' young Vic Rostrun. I fear you will be unsuccessful, but I honour your bravery in trying."

With that, he clicked his fingers, and the two guards took a pace towards Vic. It was time to leave.

The Rostruns gathered in a huddle. His mum looked Vic in the eye. "You don't have to take on this challenge; I'd rather we lived separate lives than you return and risk the wrath of Quaxitopal."

But Vic was adamant. "Look, with the help of virtual reality 'The Quest' may be possible; you see I can go anywhere and collect anything. I must give it a try."

"Virtual reality?" said his mum in an inquisitive way.

Vic replied, "There's no time to explain now, but trust me, I may be able to pull this whole thing off!"

The two guards pointed their spears at Vic to show that it was definitely time to depart.

After a quick hug with his parents he left the courtroom but paused at the doorway and gave a small wave.

"I wonder how this is all going to turn out?" Vic thought to himself.

As his parents watched their small brave son depart, they were thinking exactly the same thing.

Vic's dad looked at his wife and said hopefully, "Well, it's all down to him now. Let's hope this virtual reality stuff is not just another one of his crazy fantasies or we'll all be in trouble." Then they turned to resume their dismal duties.

The guards marched Vic along a corridor then up a narrow, dimly lit, spiral staircase. It was quite a climb and with the stifling heat Vic was soon out of breath.

When they reached the top of the staircase Vic was bemused; there didn't seem anywhere to go. The steps stopped at the ceiling!

Then one of the guards pushed his fingers into some holes on the wall and there was the grinding noise of stone on stone.

A shaft of intense white sunlight cut into the gloom. Vic raised his hands to shield his eyes from its brilliance. To his amazement, the roof was sliding open and as his eyes adjusted to the glare, he could see a clear blue sky with some birds circling lazily overhead.

The guards thrust their spears towards Vic to show that he should leave the temple. He climbed the last few steps and stepped outside. To his astonishment, he was back on top of the temple plateau. It had been hot underground, but nothing could have prepared him for the blast of heat as he stepped outside. It was like walking into an oven.

He turned around to check where the exit was and saw that the sundial with the image of the beetle had slid to one side to reveal the secret staircase. One of the guards leapt out onto the plateau and turned the beetle and the whole sundial began to slide back in place. Without a second glance at Vic, the guard jumped back down the staircase like a rabbit scampering to the safety of its warren.

"Flip!" exclaimed Vic out loud, "If I had known I could have just turned the beetle to get into the temple, I would not have had to have gone through that blinking labyrinth. Still, next time ... if there is a next time."

Vic had always been a good runner. As he was small, he often found it hard to compete in physical team games where everyone else was always taller and stronger than him. But running was a different matter. He was light and agile and on cross-country runs left the crowd of hacking coughers well behind.

Vic set off and ran like he had never run before. 'The Quest' and the fate of his parents depended on him.

Like a marathon runner intent on winning the gold medal, he headed back through the streets of the ruined city. To spur him on he imagined crowds waving and cheering the next Olympic champion.

Through the gates he sped and then with an almighty leap broke through the trees that hid city from view.

As he ran along the jungle trail, his heart pounded, and his legs felt like they were about to give way, but it was as if he was in remote control.

He had only been down the trail once before, but the trees and vines seemed familiar. They seemed to be acting as signposts to guide him back to the portal. It was almost as if they were yelling out "That way Vic!"

"It's the Guardian", he panted out loud, sure he was somehow being led.

Then, he thrust his arms into the air as he reached the finish line. There was his parents' abandoned canoe and the very welcome sight of Spike Sprite standing next to it.

"What on earth have you been up to?", exclaimed Spike, "I was wondering whether you were ever coming back, you've been absolutely ages!"

Vic was bent double with his hands on his knees, fighting for breath.

"I've been", he gasped, "In the secret city (gasp), temple (gasp), went underground and met the King (gasp) mum and dad were there, but slaves (gasp), got to complete 'The Quest' (big gasp)" and with that he fell down on his back in the undergrowth, panting hard.

He lay there gasping for air, looking up at the rays of sunshine breaking through the jungle canopy far above him.

When his breathing had just about returned to normal a small, cube-shaped head with bright blue features and unnaturally large ears came into view.

"Sounds like you had better get back and work on that Quest" said Spike Sprite, "It's not going to be easy to find the tail feather of a Quetzal bird, let alone a food that you can eat but that never runs out!"

Vic sat bolt upright and replied, "How do you know about 'The Quest'?" Then, without giving Spike the chance to speak, Vic answered his own question and whispered, "It's the Guardian, isn't it?"

Spike Sprite smiled and offered a three-fingered hand to help Vic up.

Vic grabbed the three fingers and for a second looked at the criss-crosses of thin glowing wires that made up Spike's arm.

Was this real or some crazy dream?

However, as they jumped onto the shimmering blue dot in the canoe and Vic felt the acceleration as they entered the VR tunnel, he knew this was very real.

And he sensed there were going to have to be several more virtual visits in the next few days.

VR-R

The Partnership

"Wakey, wakey!"

Vic woke up with a lurch and shielded his eyes from the brilliant sunlight. For one moment he thought he was lying on the jungle floor. He must have dozed off with exhaustion after the temple adventure and the sprint back to Spike Sprite. But then, after looking up, he realised he was back in bed at home and Nana had just opened his curtains.

"Lummy Vic, that's a really jolly pyjama top" she laughed, "I've not seen that one before!"

Vic looked down and froze.

In an instant, it all came flooding back to him. When he had got back from his trip, his main concern had been to accurately write down 'The Quest'. He had rehearsed it in his mind on the journey back, rather like when reciting your maths tables. Even in the VR tunnel, where it was hard to focus on anything but the wind whistling past your ears, he had shouted out the details.

So, on arriving home in the dead of night, he had quietly bounded upstairs and got dad's notebook out. For safekeeping, it now lay carefully hidden under the plinth of his bedside cabinet. Its poor condition meant that if it was left out, Nana could easily think it was rubbish and throw it away. That would be disastrous! Not only that, but it was just possible that if Nana looked at it, she may just work out who it originally belonged to. That would cause a lot of unwelcome questions as to where it had come from. So, the diary was always concealed.

To get at it, you had to gently lean the bedside cabinet backwards just enough to slide your hand underneath. Vic was well practised and could now get it without his alarm clock or lamp, which stood on the top of the cabinet, sliding even a millimetre.

He now acted as though the little book were sacred. He treated it with great care as he performed the daily ritual of reading it by torchlight after Nana had said goodnight.

Now it was time for him to add his own information to dad's writing and drawings. He felt a bit uncomfortable adding an entry to a diary that was not his, but 'The Quest' was an important fact about the Matapopafetal. He was sure his dad would approve, but that aside, any additions needed to be done well, like a true archaeologist recording the day's 'finds'.

Vic carefully held the book in the palm of his hand as though he was looking at a specimen of a rare butterfly. He gently opened the plain brown covers and revealed the rich colours of a sketch of a Mayan mosaic floor. Each tile had been beautifully coloured using pencil crayons. All the shaded lines were either absolutely vertical or horizontal; his dad was a stickler for detail. Now, however, it was down to Vic to focus and record the exact details of 'The Quest'. His parent's lives depended on it!

He carefully sharpened a pencil to a perfect point, as sharp as a hypodermic needle on a syringe. Then, he gently flicked through the notebook until he found the next fresh page. He recorded the date: April 17th, and then began to write down the challenges of 'The Quest' in his very best handwriting. As he wrote, he mouthed the very words King Quaxitopal had uttered. It looked as if he were in a trance.

As he completed the entry, he took a huge gasp of air and realised that he had been holding his breath. He hid the diary and flopped back on to his bed, completely exhausted.

"To complete The Quest means that Tapta Papta has come. Then the King will give up the Sacred Throne for ever."

Could he really be Tapta Papta? Could Victor Rostrun, the small boy who lived in a rundown terraced house in Eden Lane, be the one whom the Ancient Matapopafetal elders had predicted would come? Could he find the everlasting food, the feather, the goblet and present them to coincide with a black sun? It all seemed very unlikely!

With that thought buzzing in his mind, he must have fallen asleep.

So, there he now was, sitting up in bed still wearing the Mayan prisoner tunic.

"Do you like it, it's pretty cool isn't it?" he said, desperately trying to think of an explanation.

"I don't understand you youngsters" Nana replied, "One minute you want cool designer clothes the next you are choosing gaudy shirts from second-hand shops. Talking of that, out of bed this instant, you've slept in and we're due at Agnes Allsorts in half an hour!"

Vic immediately leapt out of bed to ensure that further questions were avoided. He quickly washed the jungle sweat from his body and dressed in some sensible clothes.

He then ate a monstrous breakfast; cereal, juice, a stack of hot buttered toast, and a tin of grapefruit segments, all washed down with a mug of tea.

"Gracious me", remarked Nana, "Anyone would think you ran a marathon yesterday!"

Vic laughed. It was closer to the truth than she realised.

During the morning at the shop Vic was subdued and deep in thought. There had been quite a number of bags of stuff dropped off, which for once he was grateful for. So, he quietly got on with his sorting so that Ruby Ramsbottom could make the all-important 'throw-keep-wash-display' decisions.

The truth was that his mind was on jade goblets, brightly coloured tail feathers and a very mysterious food.

While he could think of some possible ways of locating the first two items, the "promised food which though eaten will never run out" was taxing his brain.

As he sorted through a big bag of bric-a-brac, he recited the phrase over and over again in the hope of gaining inspiration. But it was like an infuriating riddle for which he could come up with no answer. Perhaps there wasn't one! The thought of failing 'The Quest', however, was something that Vic was not willing to entertain. Somehow, he just had to solve it!

His mood perked up when a friendly face poked through the storeroom curtain.

"Hi Vic, how's tricks", said Jaz as she swept in through the curtains. "D'ya like my new outfit?" She was wearing leather trousers, a leather jacket, big clumpy leather boots and dark sunglasses. It was the sort of gear that serious motor bikers with big beards and terrifying tattoos wear.

"Coooool" marvelled Vic, "You look ace!" It seemed to Vic that whatever Jaz wore she looked the biz. She was the sort of confident person who could wear the old curtain to the storeroom, and it would be a fashion statement.

"She would make the perfect partner for me" Vic thought, and he wondered if he would dare ask her about it!

"So, what's occurring VR" she asked with a knowing wink.

"There's too much to tell right now" Vic replied, "But why don't we pop out at lunchtime, there's a lot I need to fill you in on."

So, that's what they did.

Nana kindly gave them some cash and they sat down for the 'as much as you can eat' buffet at Percy's Pizzas, just a couple of doors down from Agnes Allsorts.

It was always a really popular place and Vic and Jaz had to take it in turns to serve themselves in order to avoid losing their table to the ravenous rabble that were queuing.

Seasoned diners knew the system well and watched like hawks until the next batch of fresh pizza was brought out. But there were never enough slices to satisfy everyone ready for their next helping, and there was always a mad scrum to get a wedge. In fact, it's not uncommon for customers to nearly come to blows over margaritas and meat-feasts. Small children never stand a chance in the mayhem.

What always intrigued Vic was the deserted salad cart! Carefully cut cucumber, tomato, beetroot, and grated carrot sat untouched alongside jugs of gloopy dressings.

"Not much job satisfaction for the salad slicer" thought Vic to himself as he watched Jaz jostling with a huge gentleman to get the last slice of Hawaiian Dream.

The man, called Bernard, a delivery driver from The Gristlea Pork Pie Company, a fact that Vic had noticed from the badge on his work clothes, had taken more than his fair share of the fixed price buffet. He was using his massive bulk to block one route to the serving area. He then bolted down a couple of wedges while he stood there, before taking a further two slices back to his seat. Each time he laughed with his disgusting pizza-smeared mouth, at those who had missed out.

On this occasion Jaz succeeded in grabbing the last slice just before him. Bernard returned to his seat, muttering some rude phrases under his breath.

For the next half-hour, Vic took Jaz through the visit to the lost city, only being interrupted as she leapt up to try and beat big Bernard to the next batch of pizza as it arrived at the buffet!

As Vic recounted the incredible events, Jaz's eyes grew wider making her look like a startled bush baby.

"Well, there you have it"' he concluded, "Mum and dad are alive and there may be a way of fulfilling 'The Quest' and rescuing them using virtual reality. But the challenges are tough. Jaz, I'm not kidding. If I go back and get it wrong, I'm history. King Quaxitopal was deadly serious and when I say deadly, I mean deadly!"

Jaz looked at the tomato sauce spread all over her plate and shuddered.

Vic paused and took a deep breath. This was the moment that he had been thinking about all day.

"Jaz, I've something important to ask you. Will you be my partner?"

Jaz threw her head back and laughed, "What, are you asking me to marry you?" she roared.

Vic hadn't considered the question might be taken in that way. He was about to instinctively say "Yes", especially with her sitting there in her cool biker's gear. However, he thought better of it. "Maybe in a few years, once I've got a hairy chest and have my own credit card, you'll see me in a different light", he silently thought.

"No, you twit" Vic replied, "I need a partner to help me solve 'The Quest', collect the stuff using VR and get it back to Quaxitopal. Are you up for it?"

There was a long pause, which seemed to indicate that this was all getting far too out of hand for Jaz. At the end of the day, this was going to be a matter of life and death at the hand of a ruthless Mayan King. He wasn't just asking her to go for a Sunday afternoon bike ride!

Jaz picked up her last slice of pizza and held it up high so that a long string of mozzarella cheese dangled in her mouth. Then she bit it off ferociously and declared; "You try and stop me!"

Vic beamed from ear to ear.

The pair stood up and exchanged a 'high five' while Bernard, seeing Jaz was preoccupied, waddled past to try and grab the last slice of 'Salami Slap-up'.

As they sat down, Jaz dipped her thumb in the blood red ketchup on her plate. She held it up, looked Vic in the eye and whispered - "Partners".

Vic realised what she was up to. The sauce was significant. She wanted to seal the new partnership with a solemn vow. He had learned all about promises sealed in blood in Religious Education.

This act meant they were committed to see 'The Quest' through, together, whatever happened.

He pressed his thumb against Jaz's so that the red sauce oozed out. Vic nodded and said with relief and excitement, "We're partners - even to death!" He just hoped it wouldn't come to that!

VR-S

The Strategy

The partners agreed that they needed to formulate a plan, and quick. So, they wasted no time and arranged to meet that evening to reflect on the riddles of 'The Quest'.

By the time the doorknocker of number 42 was rhythmically rapped, Vic had already got to work. He had stuck a large sheet of paper up in this bedroom, with the word 'STRATEGY' at the top. He felt that they needed a proper plan like the ones seen in darkened rooms where Generals ran their war campaigns.

So, to add atmosphere, Vic had shut the curtains and put his bedside lamp on.

He had searched high and low for a large piece of paper suitable to write 'The Quest' strategy on.

By chance, he had found a rolled-up poster at the back of his wardrobe, next to a pile of smelly sports kit and Mr Bobby Bramble, his well-loved but worn-out old teddy bear. Mr Bobby Bramble, a name which for some unknown reason he had always been called, never officially saw the light of day. However, even now he occasionally made it into Vic's bed after stressful days when Bane or Parsons had been at their worst. But, with Jaz about to arrive, this was definitely not a day for him to make an appearance, so as Vic retrieved the poster, the scraggy old bear was concealed under a stinky unwashed football shirt.

As Vic unrolled the poster, memories flooded back of where he had bought it. It had been during a school trip to the Spate Gallery in London, last year when they were studying contemporary modern art.

The picture was a hideous design of yellow, lime and orange geometric shapes. For the life of him, Vic couldn't think what inspired him to waste good money on it, but when you are on a school trip you must buy something to take home and he had plenty of pencils and rubbers already.

It was a copy of a picture called 'The Pursuit of Answers' by an artist named Ayamonthé Dole, who was a founding member of what was known as the Languid Art Movement.

According to Sir Giles Campman, the tall Tour Guide with a waxed moustache and fancy silk cravat, it was all to do with an 'expression of confusion'.

With flamboyant gestures he explained in a posh voice that it "Depicted a semester of her mid-life crisis during which she was seeking direction and enlightenment". Everyone nodded even though they didn't have a clue what he was wittering on about.

That was the infamous moment when Campman asked Alderman Roberts School group what they thought of this significant picture. In a second, Brian Bane had thrust his hand up and like a crazy parrot squawked "Gerbil jobbies, gerbil jobbies, gerbil jobbies."

Now, Bert Umber, their art teacher was normally very chilled out. In fact, in some lessons, he let the class paint whatever they liked while he sat with his pink boots up on a desk, staring into the distance with glazed eyes. It almost seemed like he was on a different planet. He was the only teacher that let you use his first name, although he did draw the line if you called him Bertram, which was the full version, or, worse still, Bertie. Best of all was his long beard and ponytail, tied up with an elastic band. It was something that 'Pop-out' Parson's occasionally made fun of in his lessons!

However, on this occasion, 'gerbil jobbies' was a step too far, even for Bert. He completely lost his temper and marched Bane off dragging him by his ear shouting "You idiot! You complete idiot!", whilst Sir Giles fumed and turned crimson.

But now, the reverse side of 'The Pursuit of Answers' by Ayamonthé Dole was about to provide a fresh canvas on which Vic and Jaz could draw their conclusions about 'The Quest'.

The name of the picture seemed an amazing coincidence as the evening was going to be spent pursuing answers about the challenge ahead. For a moment Vic looked around half expecting Spike Sprite to be there. He had grown accustomed to freaky things like this happening and sensed The Guardian was clearly influencing his life more than he realised. I mean, he had bought that picture over a year ago, long before the computer had been struck by lightning; so was this just a coincidence?

Just as Vic had finished sticking the paper up, there was a rhythmic rap on the door. He bounded downstairs to let Jaz in.

"Fancy a drink?" he asked, as she staggered through the door. "Not half", panted Jaz, "That hill seems to get steeper every time I come round!"

Vic led Jaz straight through to the kitchen, where Nana was busy hand washing some clothes and a load of beige stockings. They were hanging down from a piece of string above the sink and reminded Vic of the jungle creepers on his last VR trip.

So, with two glasses of cola, the partners went upstairs and looked at the blank STRATEGY sheet.

"What I reckon we need to do" said Vic, "is write down 'The Quest' items and any ideas we have. Then we can go and surf the Internet to work out what VR trips we need to make."

Jaz slurped and nodded, happy for Vic to take the lead.

So, down the left-hand margin Vic wrote - Jade goblet, Quetzal feather, Everlasting food, and Black sun.

"Well, what do you think?"

"The only obvious one to me is that goblet" replied Jaz, "There must be somewhere on the Net where we could find one."

"My only worry is cost" said Vic, "They can't be cheap. I think that's going to be the challenge and I don't have any savings."

"In the past, I would have stolen one for you", reflected Jaz.

Vic frowned and replied "No, we need to try and do this right, and anyway nicking stuff has got you into more than enough trouble!"

So, next to Jade goblet he wrote - "Find supplier. How do we pay?"

"The Quetzal feather doesn't bother me as much" continued Vic. "When I did the research for my Mayan project there were a few conservation sites which listed breeding programmes for Quetzal birds. They may now be almost extinct in Central America but I'm sure we can find a wildlife park where some exist. It's then just a matter of grabbing a tail feather."

"Just" laughed Jaz, "Do you think the stupid thing is going to just sit there while you pluck it?"

"Probably not" chuckled Vic, "But I once found a peacock's feather lying on the ground at a stately home, so we could strike lucky!"

Jaz didn't look convinced, so Vic wrote next to Quetzal feather - 'Locate the zoo. Hope for some luck!'

"Now here's the one that's been bugging me" said Vic, "This food that you can eat but which never runs out. I'm stumped!"

"Shame there isn't a Percy's Pizzas buffet at the Mayan city" Jaz joked.

"Yeah", agreed Vic, "So long as big Bernard wasn't there; he'd cause any amount of food to run out!"

For a few minutes, Jaz sat with her head in her hands while Vic paced around the room seeking inspiration. Finally, he was forced to put a large '?' next to that part of 'The Quest' strategy.

"And, last but not least I need to take all these things back when the sun turns black. That's another weird one!" sighed Vic.

"No, it's not", cried Jaz, "It's obvious! They mean a solar eclipse. You know, when the moon passes between the earth and the sun and blots out the light."

Vic jumped up and down. "Brilliant! Why didn't I think of that? The Maya are ace astronomers. It makes sense that 'The Quest' should be completed on such a significant day."

Next to the Black sun he wrote 'Find eclipse times coming up in Guatemala'.

Vic gulped down the remainder of his cola in one go and the bubbles stung the back of his nose.

"Right, no time to lose" he said, "Let's get surfing and find our goblet, feather and maybe even an eclipse diary, if such a thing exists."

And with that, Vic took the STRATEGY sheet down and he and Jaz rushed downstairs and booted up the computer.

Once all the icons had loaded, Vic was about to start the Internet search engine up when he noticed Jaz staring at the shimmering Guardian icon.

"I can't wait to make another VR trip" she whispered, "It feels like I'm in a dream."

Vic pinched her arm, "It's real all right; now let's find where we are going to go."

The first search for 'jade' brought up loads of websites; most relating to women by that name and showing pictures of holidays and weddings. But inputting the term 'jade goblets' was more successful.

There were a number of museum sites with historic examples, but these were of no use. However, a bit more searching revealed some international jade dealers. One site showed some sample artefacts, which included a beautiful goblet with a delicate stem.

"That's it" said Vic, "Just the sort of thing I had in mind. Now let's see, where will we be going?"

The home page was in a very strange language, which meant nothing until Vic clicked on the familiar red, white and blue flag. Then the website reloaded in English, and all became clear.

"Gracious" said Jaz, "Ho Chi Minh City in Vietnam. I never thought I'd get to go there!"

"Me neither, I've never heard of it before, but it sounds really exciting" said Vic, who was getting a thirst for travel.

He carefully saved the web address in his 'Favourites' folder to ensure he could easily find the website again and wrote the dealer's details; 'Thinna Ling's Jade Emporium' on the STRATEGY sheet.

"Now, onto the Quetzal bird" whispered Vic.

This proved an easier search as he had saved some of the sites while he was doing his Mayan project research.

He clicked on one and read out the homepage to Jaz.

"Welcome to 'The Sanctuary' Canada's world-renowned centre for the breeding of rare birds. Our skilled staff have now raised more than 300 rare species and prevented a number from extinction. These include the Lesser Spotted Parpbottom, the Fat Beaked Snoz, the Bobbing Boobie and the Long-Tailed Quetzal."

Each of the rare species mentioned was illustrated with a beautiful photograph.

"Whoa!" exclaimed Jaz, pointing at a Quetzal. "Look at that beauty. Its tail must be getting on for half a metre long."

"That would certainly impress King Quaxitopal!" said Vic. "So, it looks like we'll have to make a trip to Canada as well." He jotted the details on the wall chart.

"Now the final thing is finding the eclipse times."

This search was an instant success giving a page of options. Jaz read one out; "Dr Kat Schrödinger's Eclipse Centre … All you need to know about celestial bodies."

The site had some general pages explaining how solar and lunar eclipses occur, as well as some stunning pictures. They were so good Vic chose one to be the desktop wallpaper on his computer.

However, the most interesting bit was the on-line Eclipse Calculator. It read: "Just enter the latitude and longitude of your desired location and let Dr Schrödinger's programme calculate your next total solar eclipse."

Vic ran upstairs to his bedroom and returned within seconds with an atlas.

He furiously turned the pages until he reached Central America.

"Here we go Jaz, type in these coordinates for the capital city of Guatemala ... latitude 14° 37' N, longitude 90° 31' W."

The Eclipse Calculator set to work. Then, after an agonising wait it returned an answer.

Vic read out the details slowly, "Next total solar eclipse is on ... 21st April - I hope it's the same date in VR, but that's something we'll have to chance." Then he sat bolt upright. "Flip, that's in a few days; we're going to be hard pressed to get the stuff in time."

"Let's check when the next total eclipse in Guatemala is" suggested Jaz.

Vic hit the 'Next Eclipse' button and the computer began to process. The answer came back, and it was shocking!

Vic groaned. "We can't wait another 362 years! We'll all be long gone by then! Jaz we are going to have to get VR travelling - NOW!"

VR-T

The Feather

"Vic, we can't just go on a VR trip NOW!" complained Jaz, "I'm going to a gig later. Not only that, but I'm not dressed for a trip to Vietnam; I'd boil in this gear! And Nana is sitting next door."

It all did seem a bit hasty, but Vic was determined to start out right away.

"OK, he said "Then we'll go for the feather first. That's in Canada, which has a climate like ours, so you're dressed perfectly! And, if we give it fifteen minutes, Nana will have gone out, because it's her bingo night."

Jaz looked unsure about the pace of events but nodded.

Sure enough, Nana soon appeared in her tweed coat and 'tea cosy' hat.

"Now no getting up to mischief while I'm out, and let's hope it's my night for a full house" she laughed, as she pulled the door behind her.

Vic immediately loaded the home page of The Sanctuary and clicked on a picture of the Visitor's Centre. He glanced at Jaz and then double-clicked on the pulsating Guardian icon. Both partners held their breath as Spike Sprite zoomed down the indigo tunnel towards them.

"Hi Vic and also nice to see you too Jaz, off on some travels?" tingled Spike.

"Yep!" replied Vic "We've worked out where to get most of the things for 'The Quest' and the first stop is Canada for the Quetzal feather."

"OK", said Spike, "You both know the process."

Vic took a deep breath and placed his hand on the glass platter. As he hit the 'Scan' button, Jaz grabbed his other hand and gave it a squeeze. They both watched as the incandescent light revealed the veins in his hand and then glanced down at their feet as the agonising pins and needles began.

Jaz let out a shriek as her body became a mass of swirling 1's and 0's as they were both transformed into digital code.

In a matter of seconds, like goldfish inside a bowl, they were inside the PC looking back at the distorted image of the front room.

"Ready?" asked Spike Sprite, grinning.

"Ready!" they called out in unison.

The speed was breath-taking and as the VR destination loomed at the end of the purple tunnel all three began to run wildly in mid-air. They all landed perfectly, jogging towards the Visitor's Centre.

Spike spoke first, "I'll hide the portal beside the Visitor's Centre, down that quiet alleyway. Have fun!"

Vic soon found a Park Plan, which was divided into the continents of the world, Europe, Africa, Asia, Australasia, and The Americas.

"That's where we need to be" said Vic, pointing to the South America zone. But first we need to go here, and he pointed to a building close by marked 'Staff'. Vic set off and Jaz followed even though she didn't know what he had in mind.

Vic walked confidently into the staff area and even dared to say "Hi" to a couple of employees who were just beginning work. After a bit of searching he found a pair of doors with the sign 'Laundry' above and whispered his plan to Jaz. "We need work clothes, to blend in."

It seemed quiet, so they pushed open the doors and crept in.

That's lucky' said Vic, "There's no one here."

They found two pairs of green overalls hanging on a rail and pulled them over their clothes. Even though they were a bit big, they looked the part.

Then they returned to the Park Plan and Vic traced his finger over the map. "For South America, it's straight up here for about 400 metres, and then we turn right." Jaz nodded, and they jogged off.

On their way, they passed through Africa, waving to the ugly Fat Beaked Snoz. In Asia, the Lesser Spotted Parpbottom was making a right racket. And, as they entered The Americas, they stopped for a moment with the crowd that had gathered to marvel at the antics of the Bobbing Boobies.

There was no time to lose, so Vic and Jaz split up to search for the Quetzal bird.

After a few minutes, Vic heard Jaz shout out, "It's over here!"

He chased towards the call and joined Jaz in front of a large log cabin with Mayan images painted around the entrance.

They held their breath and walked inside.

It was hot and dark and on a concealed sound system, rainforest insects were chirping; it was remarkably realistic. Vic shut his eyes and almost believed he was back in Guatemala.

Jaz prodded him and said, "Here it is, in this huge aviary."

Sure enough, perched at the top of a tree there sat a Quetzal bird with an astonishing tail feather. Vic gazed at its beauty feeling slightly guilty that his plan was to remove the object of splendour.

"Hello! Who are you?"

Vic and Jaz turned to see a staff member standing next to them. "I'm Quentin, the Quetzal keeper" he said.

In a flash of inspiration Vic replied "Hi, I'm Vic and this is Jaz. We're on work experience?"

Quentin looked surprised, "No one told me you were joining us, I'd better check with Miss Grouch, the General Manager on my walkie-talkie."

Vic and Jaz froze.

"Hello, 1, this is 92. Can I SC two WE's in my zone. Over."

There was a crackle and silence. Quentin tweaked a knob.

"Calling 1, this is 92 do you copy, over?"

There was still silence.

"Oh well" said Quentin, "If you have uniforms, you must have got SC - I mean security clearance. Let's get to work."

Vic and Jaz looked at each other in sheer relief.

"Right Vic", instructed Quentin, "You empty the food and water trays and refill them from the trolley over there. Make sure you put plenty of banana slices out, that Quetzal loves them! Jaz, you check the floor and clear up any plops using this scoop - Miss Grouch likes it immaculate. While you do that, I'll check on the Small Toed Sponk next door. He looked really peaky yesterday."

As soon as Quentin left, Vic looked up at the Quetzal bird. It was not stupid and sensed something was on. It flapped its wings and stared at them with its beady black eyes.

Vic picked up a piece of banana and held it out. "Here Quetzal", he invited. The bird now looked really alarmed and did a massive dropping that splattered on the floor like an ice cream hitting a pavement.

"Vic, he isn't going to come near us. Put that banana down and then we'll hide behind those bushes and pounce on it when it feeds."

Vic nodded in agreement.

He placed the banana on a tree stump, and they retreated. Just then, Vic noticed a long-handled net outside the aviary. He grabbed it and then crouched next to Jaz.

They sat for what seemed like an eternity with one eye on the bird and the other looking out for Quentin.

Vic shook his head and groaned, "This just isn't working!"

Then, suddenly, there was the sound of flapping wings, and with a flash of colour the Quetzal swooped on the banana slice.

Vic leapt up and whipped the net down, but the Quetzal was far too quick. By the time Vic had got up, it was back in the treetop enjoying its treat.

"Rats! What are we going to do now?", hissed Vic in despair. Jaz shook her head.

As Vic looked out of the cage to check again for Quentin, something caught his eye. There, on display for visitors to see was a thin mahogany display cabinet about a metre long and a hands-width wide, hanging from a couple of hooks.

Vic scampered out of the cage to view the contents.

"Hey Jaz, look at this!"

There, beautifully presented, was the most amazing Quetzal bird tail feather, a good half metre long, with some blurb about its legendary secret power.

"Yes!" cried Vic triumphantly, "We'll borrow this rather than hassling that poor bird, we can always bring it back", and with that he unhooked the box.

They looked at each other thinking exactly the same thing; run! As they dashed out of the aviary they ran headlong into Quentin and knocked him to the ground.

He immediately spotted the display case they were holding and despite being winded managed to yell "Oi!"

But Vic and Jaz were long gone.

Quentin grabbed his walkie-talkie.

"Calling TEAM" he shouted, "Two visitors have taken the Quetzal feather display case ... a smallish boy and taller girl in company clothes. Stop them!"

With that, he got up and gave chase.

Throughout the park, staff began to carry out a zigzag search for the miscreants.

As they sprinted for safety, Jaz yelled "Lose the work clothes, they're a giveaway!" So they ran and leapt as if their pants were on fire, desperately trying to remove their overalls. In the process, Vic's trousers got stuck over his trainers, and so there was no option but to kick them both off.

Once back in their own clothes, and with Vic holding his shoes in one hand and the long display case in the other, they made for the Visitors' Centre.

They now deliberately walked to avoid drawing attention to themselves and it worked! Several wardens ran straight past them.

They were making good progress when they saw the 'Conservation Chuff Chuff', The Sanctuary's road-train heading towards them.

"Quick, let's get on" suggested Vic, "They'll never look for us on there." So they jumped aboard.

"Next stop, the Visitors' Centre" announced the crackly speaker.

As Vic slipped his shoes back on, he grinned at Jaz with relief and whispered, "We're nearly there."

Sure enough, the Visitors' Centre soon came into view, but to their horror a large group of workers, including Quentin, had gathered to prevent the 'tail feather thieves' leaving the park. What was worse was that they were standing near the end of the passage leading to the VR portal.

Quietly, Vic and Jaz slipped off the train and blended in with the crowd.

Vic turned to Jaz and said, "When I give the signal, sprint for the portal."

Jaz nodded, wondering what scheme Vic was hatching.

Like an inquisitive meerkat Vic stuck his head up as high as he could and looked around. He cleared his throat and, in the deepest and loudest voice he could muster, shouted in the direction of the restless green mob.

"Look, the pair with the feather are going into the Gift Shop! Quick, grab them!"

The Gift Shop was in the opposite direction to the Visitors' Centre and the diversion worked! Quentin was the first to 'take the bait', and without checking who had given the order, began to run. Then, like a row of chicks following a hen, the workers set off after Quentin, towards the Gift Shop, waving and shouting.

As soon as the green mob's attention was focussed elsewhere, Vic shouted "NOW!" and he and Jaz sprinted at full pelt towards the alley and the safety of the VR portal.

As they turned the corner, they saw Spike Sprite suddenly appear, waving them on.

They were only a short distance from the shimmering dot when a huge woman stepped out menacingly from the shadows.

"Where do you think you're going with that feather young man?" she bellowed.

Her large badge said, 'Miss Grouch, General Manager'. Her fat face was sweaty and purple with anger, or running around, or both!

"Hand it over now", she ordered, "There's no escape."

Vic and Jaz looked at each other and nodded. They were thinking the same thing. Without a moment's hesitation they split up and forced their way past her on either side.

Miss Grouch snatched wildly at thin air, missed them both and ended up giving herself a huge hug.

As she turned in anger, she saw the two friends jump on the shimmering blue dot and a strange sparkling robot standing between them. Then, before her astonished eyes, the three figures and the display case containing the precious feather suddenly turned into a mass of whirling digits and vaporised into thin air!

VR-U

The Goblet

Next morning, Vic woke up with a pain in his spine and it took a few seconds to work out why he was in agony. Then he remembered. He had hidden the Quetzal feather display case under his mattress for safekeeping. It had seemed a good idea last night but the lump it created in his bed had left him as stiff as a board!

He sat up and suddenly remembered that he arranged to meet Jaz at 11.00am in town to consider the Vietnam trip to get the goblet. He glanced at his bedside clock and groaned. It was 10.15am, he had overslept. He quickly dressed and popped his head around the door to say "Cheerio" to Nana, who was polishing the kitchen window with a scrunched-up newspaper.

"Now, you shouldn't go out without breakfast" she advised, "I made some porridge earlier. Why don't you warm it through; it will line your stomach."

Vic peered into the saucepan at the congealed grey lump.

"That'll do more than line my stomach" thought Vic, "The sheer weight will rupture it and the goop will sink into my legs." He chuckled and thought, "Perhaps that's why Nana's ankles are so fat!"

So, with a polite "No thanks", he grabbed a banana and left.

The meeting had been planned at Zero's, Vic's favourite café. He was a bit late getting there and Jaz was already reclining in one of the huge armchairs and two frothy hot chocolates sat on the table. Vic sank into the chair opposite and for a minute or so neither of them said anything while slurping the delicious drinks.

"I don't know about you" sighed Vic, "I'm shattered, but we simply have to go to Vietnam tonight."

It was a bizarre thing to say and a thin woman drinking a 'skinny soya latte' on the next table glanced at them, and then turned back to her book, pretending not to listen. Normally such a trip would require planning, not to mention a passport, which neither of them had.

Jaz nodded and remarked, "I've been awake most of the night thinking about it. Getting there is easy but paying for the goblet is the problem." Vic drained the remains of the hot chocolate and wiped the milky moustache from his top lip with his sleeve. "I haven't even got enough cash to buy us more drinks" he moaned.

They flopped back into the chairs and tried to come up with some ideas until Luigi, Zero's rather grumpy Italian manager, told them "If-a they weren't-a buying to flipping-a clear off as a-people were waiting." So, they agreed to meet up later.

At 2.30pm they sat undisturbed in front of the computer at number 42, in summer shorts and tee-shirts, putting the details together for the trip. Nana had raised her eyebrows at their dress choice; but assumed it was yet another teenage fashion statement.

After a bit of surfing, Vic found the goblet they had seen on offer at Thinna Ling's Jade Emporium of Ho Chi Minh City. It wasn't exactly a shop, but more a posh market stall which sold all manner of jade artefacts.

However, they were still no closer to working out how to pay for the goblet, so there was no option but to go into VR in the hope that things would work out.

Once Nana had settled down to watch television, Vic cheekily told her they were "Just popping down the bi-linear-digi-data-conduit", to which she smiled naively and replied, "Have a nice time love". Then, after being transformed into digital code, that's exactly what they did.

A few Vietnamese shoppers leapt in surprise as two young people and a small robot suddenly appeared from nowhere, running through the market. It was mid-evening in humid Ho Chi Minh City and the market was heaving with people; but such was the hustle and bustle that no one stopped to ask questions.

Thinna Ling's Jade Emporium was part of a vast indoor market. There were rows of closely packed shops that went on as far as the eye could see.

The place was packed with shoppers and the air was alive with the babble of bartering and buying. Animated stall owners waved madly to encourage shoppers to purchase a bargain. Some were so enthusiastic that they thrust their wares into the faces of passers-by to show the quality.

Vic stared at the peculiar range of goods on sale.

One stall displayed sacks of exotic spices, and another had hundreds of wooden boxes inlaid with glistening mother-of-pearl. Next to that was a stall selling every household item you could imagine. There was so much stuff that you could only see the top of the owner's bald head above the mound of brushes and cloths. Another stall was covered with colourful kites. But the weirdest of all had jars filled with yellow liquid and dead snakes, rather like the pickled fruit that you get at Christmas.

Vic concluded that you could probably get anything you wanted here and, hopefully, that included the jade goblet.

In the midst of the mayhem Spike Sprite yelled "Positioning the portal is going to be tricky as there are so many people. So, I'm going to hide it in that gap between the Jade Emporium and the snake stall".

Sure enough there was a narrow opening between the flimsy walls that separated the two stalls, just big enough for Vic and Jaz to squeeze down. With that, Spike disappeared.

Vic and Jaz turned to face Thinna Ling's.

The stall had a vast array of jade items from small boxes to larger carved statues presented on rows of shelves arranged like steps. They reminded Vic of the way the Maya cut terraces into hillsides to create flat land on which to grow crops.

They walked up to the stall but there was no one around. However, there was a hand bell with a sign in Vietnamese next to it. Vic assumed it meant 'Ring for attention' – so he did.

Very slowly a shopkeeper appeared from behind the shelving. He was a tiny old Vietnamese man with a face that resembled a wrinkled prune. He wore large thick glasses that magnified his eyeballs so much that they looked far too big for his face.

When he spoke, Vic and Jaz didn't understand a word, so Vic politely asked "Please, do you speak English?"

"Englush? Gosh yesh, I spick some Englash." He furiously shook Vic's hand in the hope of selling something. "My son wint to unibarsity in Lindon to study compotering. He even make a website for my jadey buznis – you's sees it?"

Vic smiled, and nodded. He felt totally ashamed that he had never mastered another language, whilst so many people in other cultures had made such an effort to learn his language.

"Now you make the bell of Ling ding, so how must I oblige you?" said the shop owner.

Jaz nudged Vic and whispered, "Ling ding", and giggled.

Vic ignored her rudeness and said, "Mr. Ling, I would like to buy that jade goblet" and he pointed to the beautiful thin stemmed cup on the top shelf.

"Ahhhh", sighed Ling "Yesh a luvervelly goblet for the handshum young gentleman". He picked it up as carefully as if he were holding a newly born chick. "Yesh, this is the very bestest one Mr Ling has hever seen. To you ... 4,500,000 Vietnamese Dong."

Jaz exploded with laughter, "First, Thinna Ling and ding and now the money is called dong."

Vic hissed at her "Jaz, it's totally inappropriate to make stupid, insensitive jokes about other cultures and people's names. Just because something is different it doesn't mean you can joke about it – now cut it out!"

Jaz looked really ashamed; she knew Vic was right.

Vic turned back to Mr Ling in utter horror, "Four and a half million" he cried, "You can't be serious!"

Mr. Ling could see that Vic had no idea how much a Dong was worth, so he whipped out a calculator. He did a quick sum and showed the result to Vic and Jaz. He beamed "Goblet costest this muchness in US dollars." It was a far smaller number of digits.

Now Jaz had been to Florida earlier that year and knew the exchange rates. "Vic, that's still really expensive, we'll never be able to afford that, not in a month of Sundays."

They looked at each other in frustration and defeat.

Suddenly Jaz's face lit up. "Work experience!" she cried. Vic looked puzzled. "Look, when we got the feather, we said we were on work experience. So, why don't we ask if I can stay here and work free of charge and then get paid with the goblet? When I'm done, you can come back and get me."

Without giving Vic a moment for discussion, Jaz approached Mr. Ling and explained their problem as simply as she could.

"Ah-ha-ha!" he replied, "You do not have the cashy and you wanna work for Ling to be gitting that goblet. It takes you weeks, but Mrs. Ling is sickly with bad heart, so help me would be good. OK, you cleany the jade, make tea drinkers and pack up each night and I tell when goblet is yours. Dealo?"

"Dealo!" replied Jaz enthusiastically.

Vic hissed at Jaz. "I need a word".

They stepped away from the stall.

"Look, Jaz, I can't leave you here; I mean, where will you live? What about food? It's crazy! Anyway, I need you around to help complete the rest of 'The Quest'".

He paused for a moment and thought.

"Look, I don't really like the idea I am about to suggest, but I think it's the only way out of this fix", and he whispered a plan in Jaz's ear. She looked concerned but nodded and for a moment they both checked and fiddled with their watches.

And, with that, Vic squeezed down between the Jade Emporium and the snake stall. Spike Sprite appeared and within seconds they had gone, leaving Jaz to begin polishing the jade at Thinna Ling's.

When Vic got back to his front room, Spike looked at him through the VDU with a concerned expression. "Vic, I don't like this - it's not illegal in VR law to leave Jaz there, but it's highly irregular."

"Don't worry Spike" assured Vic, "This is the plan. We simply must have the goblet and there was no way we could get it on that trip without money. So, this is where I need your help. I have agreed with Jaz that I will go back into VR in exactly ten minutes. Jaz and I have synchronized our watches, so she knows the exact time when we will reappear at the Emporium. At that moment she is going to make sure she is polishing the goblet we need. I need you to make sure that the portal is placed on the stall so the three of us can leap straight on and escape. But first I must write a short letter."

Spike nodded "I get the drift. It's a very unusual request, but it can be done."

Vic checked his watch.

There were five minutes to go, and he needed to write an important letter to Mr Ling. He grabbed some paper from Nana's old bureau in the front room and composed a note.

Dear Mr. Ling,

Please forgive us for leaving without paying for the goblet. It is hard to explain, but we desperately need it to save my parents lives. We are not thieves and I know that taking things is very wrong. So, I promise with all my heart that as soon as possible I will either return the goblet or bring the money to pay you back, with extra for the trouble I have caused. I do hope Mrs. Ling gets better soon and thank you.

He signed the letter, popped it into an envelope and stuck it in his pocket. He looked at his watch; one minute to go.

"Spike are you absolutely clear what you need to do?" checked Vic, "Jaz is depending on us, not to mention mum and dad".

"Crystal clear" replied Spike, "I'll sort the portal; you worry about Jaz, the goblet and that important letter."

Vic reloaded the Jade Emporium picture on the Internet.

30 seconds to go.

He placed his hand on the scanner; 19, 18, 17, 16, 15 - and then hit the scan button. As his body was transformed into a whirling mass of 1's and 0's he checked his watch. At that exact moment Jaz was doing the same.

She picked up the goblet and began to polish it; 5, 4, 3, 2, 1!

VR-V

The Food

Vic held his breath as he hurtled down the VR tunnel.

He had experienced some close shaves on his previous trips to MushyTech Inc, The Institute and The Sanctuary, not to mention with the Matapopafetal, but somehow this visit seemed even more nerve-racking. Its success depended on pinpoint timing and a fair slice of luck. He knew that within the next minute 'The Quest' could be over, for good.

Jaz had been checking her watch so much that Mr. Ling was looking at her curiously. "Your watch busted Jazzy? Itzo nearly 6.30pm. Five more minyets and we need boxing up all the jade thingeys. OK?"

Jaz nodded and calmly picked up the goblet and began to polish it with the duster that Mr. Ling had given her.

Nothing could have prepared Mr. Ling, or even Jaz, who was in on the plan, for what was about to happen.

As Jaz's watch hand clicked onto 6.30pm there was a whooshing sound and the air at the entrance to the Emporium began to ripple, just like when a stone is dropped into a pond. Jaz had never seen the VR tunnel from the other end, and it was really weird.

Suddenly, from nowhere, Vic and Spike appeared sprinting at full pelt. Within a second of them landing there was utter mayhem!

With so little space in the Emporium there was no room to slow down, and Vic and Spike crashed headlong into Mr. Ling who had come out to investigate the strange whooshing noise.

Like rugby players tackling an opponent, they accidentally shoved Mr. Ling into one of the displays. There was an awful sound of wood splitting and the shelves disintegrated. The bell on the display flew upwards dinging madly. The large green cloth, which made the simple stand look grander, came off and the three became entangled in it. To Jaz's horror, about fifty jade objects soared into the air and returned to earth like huge hailstones.

Some hit the floor, but most rained down on the mound of wrestling bodies. It was a miracle that none of them smashed.

From the bottom of the writhing pile you could just hear Mr. Ling screaming in Vietnamese. Jaz could only imagine it meant help, or call for the police, or probably something a bit ruder.

Jaz grabbed Vic's arm, and then Spike's and hauled them from the mess. That just left poor Mr. Ling wriggling helplessly in a pile of wood, material, and jade 'thingeys', like a beetle stranded on its back.

Spike turned and in an instant the portal materialised on the floor of the stall. Without a moment's delay, the three friends jumped on, with Jaz clinging to the goblet.

"Wait" cried Vic, "The letter".

He leapt from the portal, pulled a crumpled envelope from his pocket, ran over, and dropped it beside Mr. Ling, with a feeble "I'm so sorry for the trouble caused but I solemnly promise I'll be back."

He rushed back to Jaz and Spike and jumped onto the pulsating blue dot. Mr. Ling groaned and raised his dizzy head, now minus the gigantic glasses just in time to see three blurry bodies vanish before his squinting eyes.

* * *

"'Our Changing World' - that's the title of our next history project", growled 'Pop-out' Parsons. "Civilisations and societies are always changing, and I wish some of you would also change for the better, you dreadful rabble."

He scowled at Vic who had already been caught daydreaming twice in the Monday morning history lesson.

It wasn't that the lesson had been boring; in fact, the television programme on the Industrial Revolution, showing the development of bridges, steam engines and factories, had been interesting. However, the VR journey to Vietnam had left Vic exhausted, not to mention bruised, after the collision with Mr. Ling and the stall. It had been difficult to concentrate, which wasn't helped by the fact that he was still trying to work out the final part of 'The Quest'; 'a food which though eaten, will never run out'.

Parsons deliberately stood next to Vic to make him feel uncomfortable and draw his attention, and he continued.

"In the 20th century the developed world went from riding bicycles, to driving cars to travelling on rockets to the moon. History is always being made before your very eyes. Your project is to investigate how things have changed in living memory. Your task is to interview an elderly person to gain insights as to what things were like when they were a child. Make sure you get some interesting details and write it up in no more than 500 words. Have it on my desk in a week's time, or else."

Vic could have done without more homework. That week, he had already got a terrible algebra sheet for Maths and a weather recording project for Geography, as if he didn't have enough to do in trying to rescue his parents. So, as he trudged home that afternoon, he decided that the easiest solution was to speak to Nana about her life. And the fact that he was hoping to execute a daring VR rescue mission within the next few days meant that he needed to get on with Parson's project, so he decided to interview her when he got in.

Even though Nana sometimes forgot everyday things like what day it was or what she had meant to buy when she was out shopping, her memory of the 'olden days', as she called them, was razor sharp.

She loved to reminisce and talk about her childhood, so when Vic asked her to help with his homework, she was more than pleased to assist.

They sat down with cups of tea and fondant fancies and Vic had a notepad to write down details just like a newspaper reporter. Nana did not require many questions to get her going and she was soon providing all sorts of interesting details about how things were different when she was young.

"So, how was life different when I was a girl?" Nana took a deep breath and began. "Well as a very young child I lived through the end of the war. It was a hard time, but everyone pulled together and cared for each other. You actually knew everyone in the street!

I lived in a little terraced house a bit like this one. But as I was so young, I don't have many recollections about it, but I do remember that we didn't always used to sleep in the house."

Vic looked puzzled.

"Well, some nights the sirens would go off to warn us that enemy planes were on their way to bomb the city. Mother would quickly get us into our dressing gowns and rush us down the garden to sleep in what was called an Anderson shelter. It was a sort of tin shed, which was almost completely buried in the garden. Dad went to a lot of trouble to make it comfortable. There were bunk beds and wood cladding on the walls to make it cosy and there was even a bit of carpet on the floor; deep red it was. Dad often said the King's shelter wasn't as grand as ours.

It would keep you safe from the explosions if they were nearby, although you wouldn't have a chance if you got a direct hit. That sadly happened to the Carmichael family who used to go to the same church as us. Funny, most people went to church in those days.

Well, apparently, I was scared stiff about going in the shelter and Mother said I would always howl with fright. When it was morning and there had been a particularly bad raid, we would creep out wondering what on earth we'd find. On one occasion the house next door got 'firebombed' and we were lucky that ours didn't go up as well.

I can remember the boys looking in the streets for bits of shrapnel from the bombs. They used to swap them at school; not half as exciting as the stuff you have these days."

Vic scribbled the details down.

"During the war things were very hard. Most children's dads were away fighting but your great grandad was a chief engineer on the railway which was considered an essential job. That meant he didn't have to go off to fight, which was nice for us; but he didn't have it easy. The station was often bombed to stop goods being delivered. Some of his best mates got killed. After work he came home for a quick tea before going out on duty as an ARP Officer. That means Air Raid Precaution. He used to go around making sure that everyone had blackouts at their windows so there were no lights for the enemy planes to see. Lummy, he didn't half shout if someone left even a tiny crack of light showing." She giggled to herself.

"Now, I remember the gas masks. Every adult and child had one in case poisonous gas bombs were dropped. There were even ones for babies, like boxes that you could put a little one right inside."

"That must have been really scary for them" Vic added.

Nana nodded, "I remember that we used to keep our gas masks in a special box that you hung round your neck. At school they had drills to check you knew how to put them on in a hurry, just in case. We also all had identity cards. I kept mine for years until we came here when it must have got lost in the move.

There also wasn't much food available. We had things called ration books with coupons which you had to use in the shops. You would register with a grocer or butcher for normal food which was available weekly, and other fancy things such as tinned foods and biscuits were on a points system. The shop assistant would cut out the coupons for what you wanted. And, what you got had to last. If you had a roast dinner the meat had to last for days in stews and soups.

At weekends I remember my mum and I would often take an enamel can full of tea down to dad who was working on the allotment. He used to grow all sorts of vegetables and he kept rabbits in hutches too, not as pets, to eat. I never really fancied eating them because I helped to looked after them, but you didn't complain, if you did, you went without.

Now here's a funny thing. We didn't only grow food in the allotment we even grew things in the house, can you believe it, we had mushrooms in buckets under the stairs. The mushrooms used to amaze me. Dad would shake the spores from some that he had, and within a few days little white buttons were pushing up through the soil. Then, we'd pick them and the next day there were a few more. And so it went on. Sometimes they would keep coming up for days before dad had to put some fresh soil in the buckets. I remember he used to laugh and call it our fantastic food, because even though we ate it, it never ran out!"

Vic sat bolt upright and dropped his pen.

Mushrooms! You could grow them, pick them, it would look like they had all gone then, amazingly, more would come up. It was all he could do not to shriek with delight.

Nana continued.

Vic appeared to be listening, but his mind was whizzing. If he could grow some mushrooms and take them to King Quaxitopal, he could pick them, so the bucket was empty and then the next day there would be more. If Quaxitopal had never seen mushrooms before, which was a chance he would have to take, it could be enough to convince him that 'The Quest' had been completed.

"So, is that enough information?" asked Nana.

Vic beamed and replied gratefully "More than you will know."

As Nana shuffled through to make another drink, a thought shot into Vic's mind.

He rushed upstairs.

On his bedside table was a little box. He carefully opened it and there, nestling in the bottom, were some of the fast-growing super-mushroom spores, which he had brought back from his first VR trip to MushyTech Inc.

How uncanny was that? Vic grinned. He had the feather, the goblet and now he had the possibility of fulfilling the fantastic food!

VR-W

The Preparations

Grundy's Garden Centre was the kind of megastore you find on the outskirts of most towns. Vic and Nana made a couple of trips a year to Grundy's to buy bedding plants, as they were the cheapest around. Even though they didn't have much money Nana tried to keep the garden as nice as when Grandad Albert was around.

The excursions to Grundy's were painful for Vic. When Nana had to go any distance for shopping, she called for the free bright purple minibus, which the local council ran for old people. It picked you up outside your door, dropped you off at your destination and arranged a time for your return journey.

It was called the 'Out-and-About' service although young people unkindly named it the 'Wrinklies Wagon'. Vic had never lived down the fact that his mates had seen him on it on more than one occasion.

However, one good thing about going on the 'Wrinklies Wagon' was the driver, a jolly man called Ted. He always had a laugh with Vic and the old people about things they said and done, without ever being unkind. And the passengers were quick to pull Ted's leg too.

On one occasion a regular passenger and a real character called Nora, screeched "Oh heck Ted, my knicker elastic's snapped". Her baggy bloomers ended up around her ankles as she tried to get up the steps. She roared with laughter and Ted wiped away tears as he kindly turned the engine off to give Nora time to sort her knickers out.

However, despite the teasing he got from some at school, for once Vic felt glad to be with the old folks on the 'Wrinklies Wagon'. He was excited at the thought of buying a mushroom growing kit. Nana had also been surprisingly enthusiastic to get one; it seemed to spark some pleasant memories.

Grundy's was huge and sold everything a gardener could need. Not only were there countless aisles of plants and garden accessories, but books, ceramic wares, clothing and a pet centre with live birds, hamsters, and fish. There was also a coffee shop where Nana always stopped for a cup of tea and a slice of her favourite Dundee cake.

It took a few minutes for Vic to find the 'home-grow' mushroom kits especially as Nana was not too quick on her feet. Eventually they located them next to a display with a myriad of multicoloured seed packets.

The kits came in large cardboard boxes. There were a few different brands to choose from so Vic picked the most attractive and expensive looking one so as to impress King Quaxitopal. It came in a bright yellow box and was called 'Mush-Tastic'.

The kit was heavy and cumbersome, and Vic struggled to get it to the coffee shop for tea and Dundee cake, and then later on, to the till to pay. On the way home on the 'Wrinklies Wagon' it was so heavy resting on his lap that it gave him terrible pins and needles, nearly as painful as when he mutated into digital code in VR.

When Ted eventually pulled up outside number 42, Vic struggled up from his seat and wondered how on earth he was going to get everything back through VR, the jungle and to King Quaxitopal. However, as he gazed down at the 'Mush-Tastic' kit, he realised that his first concern was to get the mushrooms growing, and quick!

As soon as they had taken their coats off, Nana was as keen as Vic to get the mushrooms going. She agreed that Vic could keep it in his wardrobe, but insisted that they set it up outside, so as not to create a mess.

Vic put the mushroom kit, together with a dining room chair for Nana to sit on, just outside the back door. Once seated, he gave her the Mush-Tastic instructions which she mumbled to herself with glasses perched on the end of her nose. She looked up and smiled.

"Right-ho, this is what we need to do."

Nana slowly recited the kit preparation stages, which Vic followed to the letter. Having opened the box, Vic carefully mixed the compost, which had become compacted after being sealed inside the packaging, to form a nice soft layer. The mushroom spores were already in the soil but wouldn't activate until a special ingredient called calcium carbonate, which had to be mixed with a bit of soil and warm water, was added. However, this magic mix had to stand for fifteen minutes before being applied to the compost.

During the break, Vic gave Nana the newspaper to read and then casually went upstairs to his bedroom trying not to draw attention to himself. He opened the box on his bedside cabinet which contained the remaining MushyTech Inc. fast-growing super-mushroom spores left over from his science project. He carefully picked them all up and concealed them in his fist to ensure that the slightest breeze didn't whisk them away.

Then he sauntered back downstairs and, while Nana was engrossed in doing the newspaper puzzles, gently sprinkled the MushyTech spores over the compost, without her noticing. Vic breathed a huge sigh of relief; things were going exactly to plan. Then he sat down cross-legged by the kit and waited.

Nana checked her watch. "Times up, next stage!"

Vic spread the warm, wet calcium carbonate mix evenly over the surface of the compost making sure, as Nana had advised, that it wasn't packed down too much so as to create a microclimate in which the mushrooms would form. Neither Vic nor Nana knew what a microclimate was, but both hoped they had made one.

151

"Well that's it", said Nana, "We've set it up. Now it says that you need to leave it at normal room temperature but not in sunlight, as that can dry the compost out and kill the mushrooms. Oh, and you need to keep the surface moist, but don't over water it. They reckon that in about ten days you should see some little mushrooms beginning to grow."

Vic smiled to himself. Thanks to the genetic scientists at MushyTech Inc. he shouldn't have to wait that long.

He carefully carried the kit upstairs and placed it in his wardrobe in anticipation of a bumper crop the next day. Then, having gently shut the wardrobe door, he went downstairs and booted up the computer. He needed to double-check the times of total solar eclipses in Guatemala on Dr Kat Schrödinger's Eclipse website.

He smiled "Yup, it's definitely tomorrow at 5.00pm".

Meanwhile, in the darkness of his wardrobe, the compost had already begun to bubble and foam.

* * *

It was hard to sleep but Vic had decided not to keep checking the mushrooms, but to be patient and to wait until morning to see how well they had done.

However, the second after Vic woke up, he leapt out of bed and rushed to the wardrobe to check the crop. He held his breath and flung open the door.

"Goodness gracious!" he whispered to himself.

There, before his eyes, was a mound of mutant mushrooms. There were so many that you couldn't even see the compost. While some of the smallest ones were only the diameter of coins, there were a couple of whoppers the size of small saucers.

He punched the air in delight; he was now ready to go back to King Quaxitopal, complete The Quest and rescue his parents.

As soon as he had finished his breakfast, he rang Jaz.

"Sorry, I know it's early, but I had to ring you." He glanced round to check Nana was not listening.

"Jaz, we've done it. Last night the mushrooms sprang up like umbrellas. That means we have the feather, goblet, and food. Everything is in place; we're ready to go! We need to head off late afternoon to get back into the city in time for the eclipse, which is 5.00pm our time." He paused. "Are you up for a 4.30pm VR trip?"

Jaz laughed and said reassuringly, "Don't worry, I'll be there, I'm not going to miss the most exciting bit. I'll meet you at number 42 after school and I'll need to find some ethnic clothes for Quaxitopal."

"Good thinking, Jaz. I've got just the thing for me, that gaudy Mayan prison tunic that I brought back last time."

Before heading off for school, Vic made sure everything was in place to ensure a speedy departure into VR, to arrive in time for the eclipse. It would be a disaster to have succeeded in getting The Quest items only then to present them after the moon had silently slid across the sky and turned the sun black.

He shut his bedroom door and assembled the items on his bed.

Using a clean handkerchief, he polished the display case containing the Quetzal tail feather, the sign of great power to the Matapopafetal. It was very impressive.

Then, he wiped every fingerprint from the beautiful jade goblet, the Mayan symbol of wealth, and wrapped it carefully in the handkerchief. Both artefacts were most definitely fit for a King.

The box of mushrooms was the odd one out. It may well be the amazing food, 'which though eaten, will never run out', the Mayan sign of well-being, but a cardboard box of mega-mushrooms hardly looked like a sacred royal gift. However, he couldn't make it look any grander. The 'wow-factor' would have to be the fact that the King could pick the crop on one day and soon there would be another ready for eating. At least that was what Vic was pinning his hopes on.

Vic carefully hid all the items in his wardrobe and, for good luck, put Mr Bobby Bramble on guard in front of them.

He then set off for school.

The day seemed to go painfully slow. Vic lost count of the number of times he checked his watch. It was clear to everyone that his mind was not on the job.

Bert Umber, who was normally so chilled, had a real go at him for fidgeting during a demonstration of how to draw a bunch of bananas.

One of the lunchtime supervisors shouted at him to "Eat up as others were waiting!"

Even Miss Frale tapped him hard on the shoulder to get his attention as he gazed dreamily out of the window.

Everything seemed so pointless compared to what he was about to do, but then he couldn't blame them for not knowing. Only he and Jaz could possibly understand how seriously scary the events later that afternoon were likely to be. Even though he knew he couldn't say anything, it felt weird thinking that this may be the last time that any of them may see him if 'The Quest' did not meet King Quaxitopal's approval.

The minute the bell rang to signal the end of the school day Vic was off!

He sprinted out of the classroom, through the school gates and ran like the wind all the way home. Even though his heart was pounding fit to explode he even managed to keep running all the way up the hill to number 42.

As he reached the summit, gasping, he still managed to burst out laughing when he saw Jaz leaning on the gatepost in the most outrageous ankle length, ethnic looking dress.

She did a flamboyant twirl and said, "I found it at Agnes Allsorts today. I couldn't meet the King unless I was properly dressed, could I?"

She then practised a deep bow before Vic.

Vic checked his watch. It was 4.15pm.

"Come on Jaz, there's no time for fooling around; we don't want to keep Quaxitopal waiting. It's nearly time for the off!"

VR-X
The Off!

Vic peered round the back door so as not to reveal the gaudy Mayan tunic that he was wearing. Nana was kneeling in the garden putting in the bedding plants they had bought at Grundy's. "Thank goodness", Vic thought to himself, with Nana busy it would make the job of getting all the items for 'The Quest' downstairs and into VR easier.

He called out "Nana, don't worry Jaz and I are popping out!" She turned and waved her trowel to show that she had heard and that it was OK.

"Don't worry?" thought Vic to himself, "I'm glad she doesn't know what's going on!"

He bounded upstairs as there wasn't a second to lose. In outer space the moon was silently sliding into position to block out the sun's rays over Guatemala. The eclipse wouldn't delay if Vic was late.

Jaz grabbed the feather and goblet, and Vic humped the box of mushrooms down to the front room. He booted up the computer and loaded the image of the River Fuddi, near to where his parent's canoe had been left.

Vic checked his watch ... 4.25pm. That gave them about 30 minutes to get back to the city; that should just be possible.

He took a deep breath, clicked on the Guardian icon and Spike Sprite began to whizz down the tunnel. "Come on, come on" urged Vic.

Outside number 42 a shadowy figure crept through the broken gate into the front garden and knelt below the window. It slowly rose with just two eyes and a nose peering over the windowsill to secretly observe what was going on in the house.

"OK Vic" said Spike rubbing his metallic hands together, "I guess this is it. The Guardian's aware that you are returning to complete 'The Quest'. It wishes you well and will do whatever it can to assist you."

Vic smiled. "Thanks Spike, and please thank the Guardian next time you see it!"

Going into VR with all items for 'The Quest' was going to be tricky. With somewhat of a strain Vic could just about hold the box of mushrooms under one arm. Jaz grabbed a couple of his fingers whilst holding the goblet in her other hand and the feather case under her arm.

The shadowy observer watched the scene and giggled. How stupid Bane thought they looked in their dreadful clothes, laden like holiday makers going down to the beach.

The scanner light slowly moved under Vic's hand, which trembled as he tried to balance with the heavy mushroom box under his other arm.

The observer's eyes became startled as the two were transformed into whirling 1's and 0's, appearing for the briefest second on the computer screen before zooming away.

"Flip! So, they have gone into the computer" hissed Brian Bane. "Well I'll be ... If I hadn't seen it with my own eyes, I would never have believed it."

An evil smile spread across his face as he quickly hatched a dreadful, devious plan.

Vic, Jaz, and Spike zoomed out of the VR tunnel into the rainforest, like a row of athletes sprinting to the finish line. As experienced VR voyagers, they managed to stay on their feet, which was a good thing. With Vic grappling with the box of mushrooms and Jaz clasping the display case and goblet, they knew it would be a disaster if they had lost their footing. A tumble could ruin the items. But despite a bit of bumping into each other thankfully, everything survived the flight down the bi-linear-digi-data-conduit.

Vic put the heavy box down and for a moment the three travellers stood in the searing heat, listening to the deafening chorus of chirping insects.

"Wow" whispered Jaz as her eyes scanned the surroundings, "I can't believe this is real!"

"Well, it's all too real", said Vic checking his watch, "And we've got a job to do. If the calculations are correct, the solar eclipse will begin in a few minutes, and we need to get the stuff presented to King Quaxitopal." Vic picked the box up and was about to head off when Spike grabbed his arm.

"I'll place the portal in your parent's boat as before. Remember, it's just over there" and he pointed to the river, which was only a stone's throw away.

Vic turned and nodded. The sight of the boat made him pause. In his mind he pictured Spike, Jaz, mum, dad, and himself standing in the canoe being mutated into digital code on their way home. He hoped it was not wishful thinking. He knew that nothing was certain, and their fate was in the hands of a ruthless king.

Vic turned to Jaz. "OK partner, time to go" he said, and with that the two marched off down the forest trail with their precious load and Spike Sprite disappeared.

In the depths of VR, the Guardian viewed their progress with great interest on one of the virtual projections that surrounded it.

* * *

There was a deafening rap on the door of number 42!

Brian Bane thumped so hard that the old knocker nearly fell off. There was no answer. So, he kept on knocking for a good two minutes before finally the door opened slowly. Nana peeped round nervously, wondering what on earth all the noise was about.

"Hi, Mrs Rostrun, I'm Brian Bane, one of Vic's best mates. I've come round to see if he could help me with my algebra homework."

"Oh!" replied Nana, somewhat surprised that someone whom Vic had told her on many occasions that he disliked so much had come to visit.

"You'd better come in" said Nana in a slightly puzzled tone, "Vic and Jaz have just popped out. I expect they've just gone to the shop. Would you like a glass of cola while you wait for him to return?"

"Yes please, Mrs Rostrun. Thanks so much Mrs Rostrun." replied Bane with fake manners.

While Nana was gone, Bane took a closer look at the computer.

He whistled in disbelief.

The screen didn't look like a normal flat two-dimensional image; it was an amazing three-dimensional tunnel. It was weird. The purple colour, which went from pale purple around the outside to deepest indigo in the centre, made him feel quite giddy. The blue rectangles that converged into a single dot seemed to be drawing him in. It was almost hypnotic. He never liked the feeling of being out of control, so he shook his head violently so as to snap himself out of the mesmerising image.

"So, it's true" whispered Bane under his breath, "The stupid squirt can actually travel into virtual reality. I don't know how this thing works, or how the flip he's got this tunnel going, but there's no doubt, he and that freak Jaz are in that PC somewhere. Well Vicky, if you love virtual reality so much, maybe you'd like to stay in there."

He glanced at the door to check Nana was not coming in and then in an instant was crouching under the small table removing every cable and connection from the back of the computer. The VDU flickered and died. The hard disc stopped whirring. The green light on the top of the scanner slowly faded.

The computer was shut down!

Deep within virtual reality the Guardian sat in its hi-tech chair observing Internet and virtual activity taking place across the world. On one small area of the vast display, the Guardian noticed an area that a millisecond ago had shown an image of a rainforest with two intrepid travellers, but then which had suddenly gone black.

It pressed one of the many buttons on the arms of its hi-tech chair. Over an invisible communication system Spike Sprite's tingly voice spoke, "Yes, Guardian."

In a slow deep voice, the Guardian replied, "We have a Terminal Shut down on link 1-854A65L-A. Unless that computer is reactivated, Vic Rostrun and his companion will be trapped in VR indefinitely."

* * *

Brian Bane just managed to get back into a chair before Nana returned with a drink and some biscuits. "There you are Brian. I can't imagine where Vic's got to. I'm sure he'll be back soon."

Bane didn't say anything but glugged the cola down in one go and then forced out a huge burp that sounded like a cow mooing.

Nana winced in disgust.

"Oh well Mrs Rostrun, perhaps they aren't coming back so soon." He coughed nervously, knowing the total mayhem he had probably caused by unplugging the computer. "I'd better be getting off. I don't want to cause any bother."

"I'm so sorry Brian" said Nana kindly, "I'll tell Vic that you called in and I hope you get your maths homework finished."

As Nana closed the front door behind him, Bane thought to himself, "It's not me you should be worrying about you wrinkly old granny".

She returned to the garden to put some more plants in. After about fifteen minutes she stopped and looked up with a puzzled expression on her face.

"It's odd. I wonder where they've got to" she mumbled.

* * *

It had been enough of a challenge getting down the forest trail and through the wall of trees that concealed the lost city on the last visit, but this time, with 'The Quest' items, it was doubly difficult. It was especially hard for Vic with the heavy box of mushrooms, and as they forced their way through to the clearing a number of the fungi fell out of the box, but there was no time to pick them up.

Jaz stopped, mopped her brow, and whistled as she viewed the city for the first time. "It's magnificent", she marvelled, "Who could imagine this place exists and that there are still people living here?"

The view was truly breath-taking, and Vic put the box down for a moment to take another look at the streets, the ruined houses and the temple which towered above the other buildings in the city. It was just as he had remembered, although on his last visit it couldn't have been quite as hot because now the temple plateau in the distance seemed to be moving in the heat haze.

Vic pointed and remarked, "Jaz you see the flat area on the temple? Well, that's where we are heading and that's where the secret entrances to the underground city are. It's a bit hard to make out as it seems to be moving in the haze but ..."

Vic stopped mid-sentence.

"Hey! That's not a heat haze, there IS movement! Look, there are loads of people. What on earth are they doing out in the open?"

In an instant, the same thought came to Vic and Jaz, and they turned to each other and exclaimed "The eclipse!"

"That's it", cried Vic, "They've come out to view and celebrate the solar eclipse. The Maya are brilliant astronomers, so they must know what is about to happen."

Vic checked his watch; there were less than ten minutes to go. They had just enough time to get up to the temple square for the exact moment when the sun would turn black.

The two friends chased through the empty streets and headed for the steps up to the temple. Vic's arm muscles felt like they were on fire as he lugged the heavy box of mushrooms, but, despite the searing pain, he kept going.

As they began to climb up to the temple square the air began to cool. It was weird, it was also getting darker and, not only that, but everything was also getting quieter. The insects had stopped chirping and there were no birds circling and calling out overhead.

All of nature sensed the wonder of the eclipse about to take place.

In the nick of time Vic and Jaz reached the top of the steps and walked out onto the temple square. There before them were about fifty people kneeling silently in a triangular formation on the ground. It looked as though they were praying.

Vic could see that King Quaxitopal was kneeling at the point of the triangle in his finest royal gowns.

Vic looked up at the sky and squinted. The moon now appeared to be covering half of the sun and an eerie shadow fell over the land.

In the loudest voice he could muster he cried out "King Quaxitopal. I'm back, and I have completed 'The Quest'.

VR-Y
The Eclipse

Every eye was fixed on the extraordinary solar eclipse. The moon precisely covered the sun and the bright corona of the sun's light blazed around the black disc. It was a fitting moment for 'The Quest' items to be presented. Despite being morning in Guatemala, it was eerily dark with a distinct chill in the air.

Vic shivered.

King Quaxitopal slowly walked over to him and indicated for Vic's dad to join them to translate.

"The King commends you for your wisdom in returning when the sun turns dark. There is only one wise elder left who can predict the heavenly movements, Quaxitopal is amazed that you possess the skill. Have you brought 'The Quest' items?"

Vic nodded.

The King roared a command and his kneeling subjects leapt up and started making an incredible chanting noise. They formed a circle around Vic and Jaz; there would clearly be no escape if 'The Quest' items were not to the King's liking.

Vic watched as two of the oldest, most wizened men that he had ever seen, hobbled across the temple plateau to the sundial with the beetle on. They twisted the stone insect and the sundial slowly slid to one side, just as when Vic had been driven from the underground city on his last visit. The two men disappeared down the spiral staircase.

Vic's dad whispered "They are the wise elders, the next most powerful citizens to the King. The legend of Tapta Papta states that the elders must receive 'The Quest' offerings on a sacred golden platter."

Vic's eyes focussed on the sundial. After what seemed like an age, the two baldheads reappeared. The Maya stopped their chant and clapped rhythmically while the elders placed a large golden tray covered by a beautiful, embroidered cloth at Vic's feet.

The King then gave a majestic speech, which Vic's dad translated.

"The ancient elders foretold that a pale-skinned warrior would one day come. This great warrior, called Tapta Papta, would bring great riches, power, and everlasting food. It would mark a time of never-ending prosperity. 'The Quest' requires signs to be brought.

For wealth: a carved goblet of finest jade.

For power: the tail feather of the Quetzal bird.

For well-being: a food, which though eaten, will never run out.

If 'The Quest' is completed, the King will give up the throne forever. The time has come to test whether you are Tapta Papta. Present your sacred offerings!"

The King whisked the embroidered cloth from the golden platter to reveal a small golden statue encrusted with jewels. Beside it was a deadly looking golden dagger.

At that moment, the moon began to slide past the sun and the first rays of sunlight glinted on the jewels and the razor-sharp edge of the blade.

Vic's dad continued speaking, "If 'The Quest' items are acceptable then the King and elders will kneel and present you with the 'Sacred Statue of The Quest'. If 'The Quest' items are unacceptable ...". His dad paused.

Vic nodded. He didn't need for his dad to finish; he got the gist from the ceremonial dagger, glinting on the tray.

"This is it, Jaz" whispered Vic, and he took the goblet and feather from her.

With as much grandeur as he could muster, he raised the goblet to the sky and then slowly placed it on the platter. In a loud voice he cried out "I bring you the goblet of wealth".

Next, he raised the feather in the display case above his head and then, bowing low, placed it alongside the goblet on the tray. "I present the Quetzal feather of power".

When the Mayan saw the feather, they gasped and began to chatter. King Quaxitopal held up his hand for silence.

"Finally" announced Vic, "I bring you the sign of well-being, a food which though eaten will never run out." To make the very ordinary looking cardboard box of mushrooms look mystical he shut his eyes and shook violently as he placed it on the platter.

From behind him, Vic heard his dad hiss "Mushrooms! I can't believe it. You've brought a box of measly mushrooms? We're doomed!"

Vic turned and tried to assure him "It was all we could think of but trust me these ones aren't normal."

The King and elders approached the platter and inspected the offerings. They nodded in wonder at the impressive goblet and feather. However, they were suspicious at the sight of the food. One of the elders reached out a finger and touched the largest mushroom. He quickly pulled his finger away as though the fungi might bite him.

The King spoke to Vic's dad, who translated. "They accept the excellent goblet and feather, but you must explain the food."

Vic had feared that the mushrooms could be a problem, so there was nothing left to do, but provide a demonstration.

"Oh, Matapopafetal" he said confidently, "I bring you a rare delicacy from across the oceans ... mushrooms."

The King frowned, then turned to the people and declared; "Marshy-humes".

The Maya looked at each other, puzzled but intrigued.

Vic continued, "While some mushrooms are deadly poisonous, these are edible and delicious. They make a super salad and are fabulous when sautéed with steak. They are truly incredible as once they are picked others will soon grow, without the need for more seeds."

With that, Vic picked one and ate it. It was bland, but he gave the impression that it tasted like the most expensive chocolate on earth.

"O King, let me pick the mushrooms and place them on the sacred platter to make room for the next amazing crop to come forth."

The King listened to Vic's dad's translation and then nodded.

One by one, Vic plucked the mushrooms giving each a good shake to make some spores fall back into the compost. The mushroom mound on the platter increased in size. Vic saved the largest and finest fungi until last and placed it on top of the heap with great ceremony.

Now, Vic had thought that they may have to stay in the city overnight to wait for the next crop to grow, but nothing could have prepared him for what then happened.

Before everyone's eyes, the compost began to swell and heave as if it had a life of its own. Then, as if moved by an invisible trowel, the soil stirred, and small white domes erupted through the rich compost.

The genetic technology of Mushy Tech Inc. was unbelievable. The next crop of mushrooms had obviously been ready to pop up but had been held in place by the sheer weight of the first crop above. In a matter of seconds new mushrooms suddenly sprouted into life like umbrellas being opened.

Everyone gasped; it was truly amazing.

The King was astonished and signalled to the elders to join him for a discussion. Vic looked round at his parents and gave them a hopeful 'thumbs up'.

After a short debate, the King returned looking vexed. He spoke to Vic's dad who relayed the conclusion.

"Young man, it is true that you have brought items that seem to fulfil 'The Quest'. You have shown great insight in arriving when the sun turned black. However, our ancient drawings show Tapta Papta as one who is far older. We do not believe that you can be the chosen one to become our ruler, but that your powers must come from some other unknown source."

Even though the King was right, Vic butted in. "Hey, that's not fair! I have completed 'The Quest'. You must honour your word."

Vic's dad grabbed his arm "Steady son, let me finish."

The King nodded for Vic's dad to continue.

"However, as you have demonstrated truly mysterious abilities and immense bravery for a small boy, I agree to release your parents, it's a just reward. You are all free to go!"

Vic punched the air in delight.

Whether they thought he was Tapta Papta or not didn't really matter; he had got the result he had dreamed about.

The King turned and gave a command to the people, who all knelt and bowed with their faces to the ground. "This is their customary way of bidding goodbye" explained Vic's dad, "We must do the same".

The Rostruns and Jaz bowed by the golden platter.

Vic's dad then whispered, "Come on, let's get going."

They didn't wait a second longer, but quietly got up, walked briskly away and down the temple steps leaving the Mayans still bowing on the ground.

"OK, where to?" enquired Vic's mum.

"The VR portal is positioned in your old canoe, by the River Fuddi" directed Vic, "Come on, it shouldn't take long".

Vic's parents looked bewildered, but after the mushroom incident they had no option but to follow obediently.

As they began to wind their way through the deserted streets Vic's mum glanced back over her shoulder.

"I don't know why, but I've got a bad feeling. I don't trust Quaxitopal, so let's get a move on."

So, with that, they began jogging back to the canoe.

*   *   *

There was a loud rap on the door of number 42. Nana picked up her knitting and went to answer assuming that Brian Bane was back with his algebra problems. But, to her complete surprise Collingwood filled the doorframe.

"Hiya Nana, I bet you didn't expect me! Sorry I didn't call, but I had to come over on urgent business at the last minute. I hope you don't mind. I not staying, but I thought I'd call in all the same and see how you and VR were doing."

"Collingwood, you're always welcome" replied Nana, "But there's one problem!' Collingwood looked worried. "I haven't got any cola" laughed Nana, "But I can offer you a nice cup of tea and some donuts."

"Donuts yes, but tea no; however a nice glass of milk wouldn't go a miss! So, where's VR?" enquired Collingwood.

"Oh, he's popped out with a friend, they should be back soon" said Nana as she padded off to the kitchen.

"Well if you don't mind" said Collingwood, "While we're waiting, I wouldn't mind using the Internet to check my emails, stocks and shares." With that he went over to the PC and switched it on.

Nothing happened.

"What the heck!" remarked Collingwood.

He crouched on the floor and checked to see if the electric socket was switched off at the wall. "Great balls of fire, what's VR been up to?" he cried, "Every jolly cable is disconnected!"

He crawled further behind the PC and began to plug each cable in the correct sockets.

Nana returned with the pile of donuts and the biggest glass in the house, filled to the brim with milk. "There you go" she said kindly, "What on earth are you up to?"

Collingwood grunted and squeezed back out from under the table, followed by some fearsome farts. "I don't get it. The PC has been disconnected. I told VR not to mess with it, but I've fixed it and I'll fix Vic when he gets back" he joked.

And with that he helped himself to the biggest donut.

* * *

They could have only been about fifty metres from the VR portal when Vic heard a whistle in the air. Then, there was another that sounded even closer, followed by a thud in a nearby tree. An arrow quivered in the trunk.

"Run!" yelled Vic's dad, "You were right Alice that tyrant has changed his mind, now they're coming after us. He wants to make us all slaves, especially after Vic's display of power. Quick Vic, you'd better get us out of here fast."

Vic sprinted off towards the boat with the rest of the group in hot pursuit. To his relief, and his parent's astonishment, Spike Sprite was there waving madly.

"Vic" yelled Spike, who for the first time ever seemed in a real panic. "Disaster! The VR portal cannot be accessed. There has been a terminal shut down on your Internet link. Someone's turned your computer off. Now we're all trapped here!"

At that very moment about twenty Mayan warriors appeared simultaneously from the jungle around them. With poisoned arrows drawn on their bows they quickly surrounded the group. One of them let out a long shrill whistle and everyone stood in silence, eyeing each other nervously.

Within seconds King Quaxitopal, the elders and even more warriors became visible, marching down the jungle trail.

Vic's dad turned to the group. "Unless anyone's got a bright idea, I think we may be done for!"

VR-Z

The Homecoming

In the front room of number 42, Collingwood devoured a donut in two bites and connected to the Internet.

* * *

King Quaxitopal approached the quivering captives. He was about to issue an order to the warriors when he stopped and gasped. A bright blue pulsating dot appeared in the bottom of the boat, which expanded quickly until it was about a half a metre across.

The brave Mayan warriors cried out and retreated from the boat. King Quaxitopal took a pace back and hissed something to Vic's dad.

"Vic, he wants to know what it is" said his dad, "Come to that, so do I!".

"Trust me dad. Just translate and don't ask questions" advised Vic. Then he instructed the others "While I'm talking, everyone calmly hold hands."

"Your Majesty" began Vic in a bold voice, "Even though I completed 'The Quest' you doubted that I was Tapta Papta. As a sign of my great displeasure, I have drawn energy from the mighty planets to make this sign appear before you. Be warned that this cosmic circle can transport anyone to a distant place in the universe in an instant."

Vic's dad translated the speech.

As the Mayan warriors trembled uncontrollably, the row of friends quietly joined hands as Vic had instructed.

Vic continued. "O King, you and your warriors must now bow before me and beg for mercy."

Vic's dad translated. Within a split second every Mayan, including Quaxitopal, were laying face-down on the jungle floor quivering in fear.

Vic turned to the group, smiled broadly, and said, "Hold tight everyone, we're going home."

With that he grabbed his parent's hands, jumped into the boat, and stood on the blue dot.

From his position on the ground, King Quaxitopal heard a strange whooshing sound. He lifted his face just enough to peep at the group and whimpered as they turned into a cloud of 1's and 0's.

As the whooshing sound got louder, Quaxitopal shook violently, wondering what would become of him at the hands of the mighty Tapta Papta. Then, with a shrill whistle, the noise stopped. After a few seconds every Mayan head looked up slowly from the blanket of leaves and stared at the boat.

King Quaxitopal cried out in utter surprise. They had gone!

* * *

Deep within virtual reality a siren sounded, and a voice spoke: "Warning! VR cloning now taking place on link 1-854A65L-A. Two adults emerging from VR into the real world in which they also exist. Real world location displayed on Screen X1. Emergency procedure must be initiated."

The Guardian turned from scanning millions of Internet images and focussed on Screen X1.

There was a map of Central America, rather like a satellite view on a weather forecast, with a flashing dot in Guatemala. The Guardian pressed a button on the arm of its hi-tech chair and the image zoomed in with amazing speed. First, whole cities and forests became visible. Then a dense jungle area. Then a clearing in the jungle and a deserted city. Then, incredibly, the view went below ground, to a hidden room.

The Guardian viewed the scene. Sure enough, there were Vic's parents existing in the real world, not virtual reality from which they were about to emerge, serving a lavish meal to King Quaxitopal.

If the Guardian did not act immediately, Vic would soon have two sets of parents; one just about to exit VR at number 42 and the other still held prisoner within the real lost city deep in the jungle.

The Guardian had to prevent VR cloning at all costs. The course of history could be changed if extra human beings existed on the earth.

It pulled out a small remote control from its hi-tech chair and pressed some buttons. The voice spoke again "Emergency procedure activated. Two adults existing in the real world will be deleted in 5 seconds - 4, 3, 2, 1."

The Guardian watched Screen X1 intently. Suddenly, in the real world just as Vic's mum was pouring a goblet of wine for the King and his dad was offering a platter of fruit, they turned into a whirling mass of 1's and 0's and disappeared.

The Guardian spoke. "Cloning averted. Two adults now leaving link 1-854A65L-A no longer exist in Guatemala."

No-one should underestimate the power of The Guardian!

* * *

Vic roared with laughter as the group zoomed down the VR tunnel. He could hear his parents shrieking. It was the kind of embarrassing parental behaviour that normally made him cringe. On this occasion, however, Vic wasn't bothered; it was just great to know they were there.

Then, in the distance, a spot of light appeared and within a second, they were bobbing around in the computer monitor looking out at the front room of number 42.

Vic's dad was the first to speak. "Well I'll be! We're inside a computer and would you believe it, Collingwood's looking at us through the other side of the screen?"

Sure enough, Collingwood's fat face was staring in shock at a group of tiny people floating around inside the computer monitor, right in front of his bulbous nose. He leapt in surprise and then rushed out of the room only to return a few seconds later dragging Nana behind him, still holding her knitting with the wool unravelling behind her.

The two then peered at the computer screen. Collingwood shook his head and knocked on the monitor to check that he wasn't dreaming. To the VR travellers, the tap was deafening, and they all yelled and held their ears.

"Come on" said Spike, "It's time for you to leave VR and say a proper hello!"

In the front room, Collingwood and Nana watched in utter disbelief as the air began to ripple and then a loud whooshing noise filled the room, followed by a mass of whirling 1's and 0's.

Nana cried out "Oh lummy, Collingwood, the Instant-Net's gone bonkers, do something before it explodes!"

In terror, Collingwood leapt towards the computer, but before he could get to the power switch Vic, his mum and dad and Jaz materialised.

For a few seconds no one said anything, but simply stared at each other. Then the VR travellers cheered wildly.

Seeing everyone reunited was too much for Nana, she went all wobbly and fell in a heap in the chair. Collingwood stood in a trance with his eyes wide open, repeating the phrase "Jumping Jehoshaphat!"

Thankfully, Vic's mum took control. "Right, everyone calm down and Collingwood for goodness sake get a grip. Now Vic, please explain what on earth is going on, we're all fascinated."

So, everyone sat down apart from Vic, who took a deep breath and began.

"It's all about VR! Not me, but virtual reality. That's what you can see on the computer", and he pointed to the tunnel and Spike Sprite, who waved back from the screen.

A few weeks ago, Collingwood did the kindest thing. I was doing badly at school, but then I found this book at the charity shop and explained to Nana that everyone now does their research on the Internet.

Well, unbeknown to me, Nana spoke to Collingwood. On his next visit he turned up with this lovely computer. At first it was just a normal PC, but a few days after getting it, the house was struck by lightning during a terrible storm. I stood and watched as a lightning strike crackled all over the machine. Nana was hiding under the stairs, and she didn't see what happened. Anyway, I thought it had ruined the computer as it was too hot to touch. But, on closer inspection, it seemed OK, except there was a weird new icon on the screen that said Guardian."

Collingwood looked intrigued and said, "So, what the heck is that?"

"Well", continued Vic, "Later that night, when Nana was asleep, I came down and doubled clicked on the icon. That activated the VR portal. Spike Sprite came down the purple tunnel and told me how a virtual world, an exact copy of the real one, existed on a secret chip in the computer. Normally you can't get access to it. However, if a computer suffers a huge blast of electricity called a spike, the virtual world is unlocked. Well, our electrical lightning blast was the largest ever known ... 9.15 mega-sizzles!

Now, the VR portal was set up I could travel inside the computer. I could visit any virtual location using an image from the Internet to set the destination. You get into VR using the scanner to scan your hand, which transforms you into digital code.

Well, I thought I must be dreaming. It sounded too wacky to be true, but I tried it out and it worked!

On my first trip I visited a laboratory called Mushy Tech Inc. and collected some fast-growing mushroom spores for a science project. Mind you, I nearly got caught by a giant scientist with tweezers."

Vic's mum frowned.

"After that I visited the World Institute for Objects of Antiquity, to take a look at where you worked. I went one night and had a good look around Professor Uralt's office. Well, I found dad's diary in his filing cabinet and brought it back. It showed where you had been and information about the lost city. I then realised that a crumpled bit of paper that I had left in your file had the code to open the secret temple door, so Jaz and I went back to get it.

That set me up for the VR visit to the lost city. Using your diary, I opened the temple door and made it through the scary labyrinth, narrowly avoiding getting eaten by huge snakes. Well, then I found mum and dad, but King Quaxitopal wouldn't let them go unless I completed 'The Quest of Tapta Papta'.

I was sure that using virtual reality I could find the Quetzal feather, the goblet, and the amazing food. Jaz helped me - she's been brilliant. We got the feather from a bird sanctuary in Canada and the goblet from Mr Ling, a jade merchant in Vietnam.

It was Nana who solved the problem of the amazing food. She was helping me with a history project about life during the war and told me about the mushrooms the family used to grow under the stairs. Even though she ate them, more mysteriously came up. It seemed to solve 'The Quest' riddle, so we bought a 'grow your own' mushroom kit from Grundy's.

Now in some strange way, the Guardian, the amazing being who looks after virtual reality, helped to guide me in completing 'The Quest'. I'm not sure how it does it, but wacky coincidences happened, such as finding the fast-growing mushroom spores that turned out to be the amazing food.

Anyway, having got all 'The Quest' items, it was then just a case of taking them back on the day the sun turned black. Jaz worked that one out. We found the solar eclipse dates for Guatemala on the Internet and returned exactly at the right time to complete the challenge and rescue you.

The only bit I can't work out was why the VR portal failed as we were about to escape."

At this point Collingwood chipped in. "I think I might be able to shed some light on the portal failure. I arrived here less than an hour ago and tried to get onto the Internet, but all the wires were disconnected; it was a right old mess. So, I plugged all the leads back in and was surfing the web, when suddenly the screen went weird, and you all arrived."

"It must have been that dreadful burping Bane lad" said Nana, "He came around earlier and somehow I thought he was up to no good."

"Well" said Vic's dad, "This is hard for any of us to take in, but here we are, reunited at last. And it's all thanks to VR; the mighty brave, clever and resourceful Vic Rostrun, and the mind-boggling virtual reality. Oh, and I forgot to mention, there's another VR which we need to be grateful for!"

Everyone looked curious.

Vic's dad slowly pulled a solid gold, jewel encrusted statue from under his Mayan tunic.

"It's the one that was on the platter at 'The Quest' ceremony. I managed to grab it as we were escaping", he laughed. "I think after everything that evil king put us through, we more than deserved it!"

"So, now we certainly are VR ... Very Rich!"

Postscript

(An extra piece of information about an event after it's happened.)

As you will have gathered from the account Vic is a good lad. So he did return to 'The Sanctuary' in Canada where he made a significant donation to support the conservation work which more than made up for the quetzal feather, he took. Thankfully, the dreadful Miss Grouch had left and apparently gone to work with warthogs, which Vic thought was a good match.

Vic and Jaz also returned to 'Thinna Ling's Jade Emporium' and paid Mr Ling double the price for the jade goblet. He was delighted and even though Vic recounted the story, Mr Ling failed to fully grasp the events that had taken place. They all became great friends and often on a weekend Vic and Jaz popped back to help Mr Ling and his family. And Vic even learned to speak a little Vietnamese.

So, all's well that ends well!

Can you imagine what Vic and Spike Sprite are up to right now? If it's mind-blowingly amazing, then you are probably right!

www.ingramcontent.com/pod-product-compliance
Lightning Source LLC
Chambersburg PA
CBHW070948050326
40689CB00014B/3395